THEATRE
OF THE
SPIRIT

THEATRE OF THE SPIRIT

A Worship Handbook

Rey O'Day
Edward A. Powers

The Pilgrim Press
New York

Library of Congress Cataloging in Publication Data

O'Day, Rey, 1947–
  Theatre of the spirit.

  Bibliography: p. 193
  1. Public worship.   I.   Powers, Edward A., joint
author.   II.   Title.
BV15.3   264'.05834   80-14165
ISBN 0-8298-0363-7 (pbk.)

For acknowledgments and sources, see Notes, beginning on page 185.

Unless otherwise indicated, biblical quotations are from the *Revised Standard Version of the Bible*, copyright 1946, 1952 and © 1971 by the Division of Christian Education, National Council of Churches and are used by permission. The scripture reference identified JB is from *The Jerusalem Bible*, copyright © 1966 by Darton, Longman & Todd Ltd. and Doubleday and Company, Inc. Used by permission of the publisher. The excerpt marked NEB is from *The New English Bible*. © The Delegates of the Oxford University Press and the Syndics of the Cambridge University Press, 1961, 1970. Reprinted by permission. Quotations noted KJV are from the *King James Version* of the Bible. The scripture quotation marked PHILLIPS is from the revised edition of *The New Testament in Modern English* by J.B. Phillips and is reprinted with permission of Macmillan Publishing Company, Inc. © J.B. Phillips 1958, 1960, 1972.

Photo Credits:

Luoma, 1; *A.D.* magazine, 10, 67, 83D, 106B,D; John A. Gibson Jr., 26; Religious News Service, 45, 76D, 83A,B, 106A,C, 135, 141, 149; Ross Clark, 51; Charles E. Dilsner, 76A; John Moynahan and Co., 76B; Walden, 76C; Bob Walker, 83C; Commission on Ecumenical Mission and Relations, UPC USA, 86; *Presbyterian Life* magazine, 94; Ken Thompson, 98; John F. Kleinman, 119; Don Heath, 122, 127.

The Pilgrim Press, 132 W. 31 Street, New York, New York 10001

Contents

Preface

In ways that are sometimes similar and other times diverse, we experience worship in the core of our beings. It is part of the substance of our lives.

Rey O'Day is a dancer, choreographer, entertainment manager and producer, earthy mystic, feminist, and teacher. Ed Powers is an educator, administrator, planner, doer, philosopher, preacher, and literary artist. Both of us celebrate life and love deeply and both of us care enormously about worship. We want to experience it where it is done creatively, authentically, and effectively; therefore, we write this book out of the urgency of our own experience. Since we humans will worship someone or something, whether well or badly, we need to be intentional about the character of our worship.

Rey is a member of the Woodland Hills Community Church (United Church of Christ) in the Los Angeles area. Ed is a member of Judson Memorial Church (American Baptist and United Church of Christ) in New York City. Both of these are vital, worshiping congregations that have taught us much about the meaning of worship, its aesthetics, and its action.

We have often led and been led in worship. Our convictions are strong about what works—worship that enhances our sense of awe, wonder, contrition, reconciliation, hope, power, promise, dedication, and mission. We have equally strong convictions about what does not work—worship attempts that are sloppy, unimaginative, irrelevant, inauthentic, and that blunt human possibilities.

We are Christians, and our sense of worship is rooted in that tradition. To be "rooted" is not to be "stuck" in a tradition but to be nourished in creative ways from its wellsprings. We try to do that in this book.

Our convictions and experience are rooted in the Bible. It is the book of our family and the family of faith. We want to see it come alive for people—so that it becomes the "living" Word.

We desire to develop worship approaches that are rooted in the

Christian tradition, enhanced by the arts, and developed so as to nourish the spirit and enable us to catch a fuller glimpse of an androgynous God and our full humanity. This book is directed toward that end.

Rey O'Day
Edward A. Powers

Worship—The Work of the People. . . . The phenomenon of worship is a universal human experience which is not done to us or for us but with us.

CHAPTER 1

The Work of the People

The phenomenon of worship is a universal human experience. One way or another, each of us and each people worships someone or something. We see the evidence in King Tut's artifacts of thirty-two centuries ago; in the caves of ancient people; and in the perennial symbols of life and death, in fear and hope, in giving birth and renewing life, in mysteries of seasons and growth, in the awesomeness of seas and mountains, and in the wonder of being female and male.

Today's expression of that universality may be seen, in part, in the reach toward Eastern religions by many young people, in the new emphasis on the charismatic and the resurgence of evangelical movements, in the almost cultic ritual of jogging, and in interest in signs of the zodiac. Gallup poll respondents consistently report their belief in God. A survey on unchurched Americans, released at Eastertime in 1978, revealed, basically, that the unchurched were firm believers in God and that they accepted many elements of Christian doctrine as well.[1]

Definitions of worship abound: it is our ultimate concern; it is the reaching out of the human spirit for the Loving One and the loving community; it is the "search of the creature for the Eternal,"[2] to use Evelyn Underhill's fine phrase.

Paul S. McElroy says of it:

Worship is important and difficult. It is an attempt to make clear the reality and nearness of God to the end that God may be able to do for us, in us, and through us, and so for the world-at-large, what . . . [God] desires. That is why the greatest discoveries yet to be made will be along spiritual lines and by means of worship. The more meaningful worship becomes the more clearly will we realize that material

2

things do not bring happiness and are of little value in making us more creatively powerful. Whether worship be expressed in private prayer or in corporate observance, it involves the whole of life.[3]

The Work of the People

The term liturgy (the Greek word is *leiturgia*) literally means "the work of the people." That is very instructive. We often think of liturgy as a piece of worship or the worship service itself and that is accurate; but underneath it all is the core meaning—the work we do together. To describe it as work is not to violate the sabbath, but to understand worship as something we do, something creative and expressive. We expend our energy to make it happen. Liturgy is not something done to or for us but with us.

To claim it for the people is to understand its corporateness (the Latin word *corpus* means "body"). We're in this together. There are, of course, solitary prayers and individual acts of worship, and, God knows, they are authentic and important. Yet, one cannot worship for another. Luther was clear about this in saying that we must do our own believing, as we must do our own dying. Further, to be Christian is to enter into a caring body so that even in our solitariness we are part of the body of Christ. We the people together adore, seek, confess, love, serve, share, hope, pray, and wonder. We do it with elements that become familiar and workable, using forms that have deep roots in the earliest synagogue, Jesus' time, the catacombs, the Reformation, or the American frontier.

Worship is our work together as the people of God in this place—gathered and scattered. Some people feel that they can worship and be good Christians in their solitariness, but it just doesn't work that way. In work, learning, recreation, or politics our individuality is enhanced by participation in a group or team. So it is with worship. We learn from one another. Our separated and broken relationships are made whole in the community of faith. We are Christians in relationship, not in solitariness. Together we discover new forms, new ways, and new symbols through which to express our worship.

There is a link between the concerns of leisure and the nature of worship. To be engaged in leisure is not just to be at rest. It is to have the mind and spirit engaged in a different mode and style. When we are in touch with our aspirations, our tired, work-plagued bodies are renewed, made whole.

Leisure is a participatory reality. It is active. It is embodied. To be humanized by it, one cannot simply observe. So it is with worship. It is getting in touch with our deepest roots. It is like a plane soaring on wind currents, except in worship it is the currents of the spirit. It is a cleansing and focusing of the mind.

Worship, like leisure, is an activity we choose to share in. It is one form of the restorative, creative use of free time. It is the ennoblement of the discretionary. Thus, worship and leisure are not competitive realities. Worship contributes to the meaning of leisure. Worship activities take place during our leisure time.

There is a close correlation between the qualities of a congregation's worship life and its growth, whether measured in quantitative or qualitative terms. Worship fuels and feeds the life of the congregation. It is square one: the basic nurturing matrix through which the spirit of the people develops.

Church growth studies clearly show that both new growth and the vitality of the present membership are directly correlated with the quality of worship. Edward K. Perry, commenting on a study of Presbyterian churches in upstate New York, contends that "no congregation grows unless its worship is a positive, uplifting and moving experience; and, every congregation that I know that is in 'growth trouble' . . . has something wrong with its worship life."[4]

David A. Roozen concludes his statement on the direct correlation of worship and growth by saying, "What is important . . . is the quality of worship and the degree to which the worship meets the expectations of the congregation."[5]

Theatre of the Spirit

Consider how revolutionary it is to say that we are the actors and God is the audience. Both actor and audience are essential to the play's performance, the work of theatre. Defining God's role as audience is not a passive statement. An audience can stamp its feet, clap its hands, cheer, sigh, gasp, or laugh as the action continues. An audience is alive, breathing, and responsive to the performers. And an audience can walk out on a lousy performance.

The actor/theatre metaphor may lead us down some false byways. We do not mean to suggest "play acting," embracing a role that is not one's own. Nor do we assume that everything is cut and dried, so that one only needs to follow out a script. The theatre is "of the spirit," calling upon all our resources of dramatic statement, personal authenticity, risk, and interaction with the Audience.

But saying that we all are the actors makes a radical difference in how we all perceive ourselves and behave. We are active participants. We enter the narthex or the side door and suddenly we are onstage. To be sure, there are prompters, but the action is ours. We begin with a spirit of quietness and of expectation as the setting and presence begin to get to us. We contemplate what we bring to these moments—our needs, hopes, yearnings, and gifts. Inevitably, we are led to pray for and care about others—some of whom catch our eyes as we glance around the room and some of whom are not there.

The prelude is not just a warm-up or "cover" music. It is a medium of communication and linkage. The call to worship and the invocation provide us the opportunity to get in touch with the awesomeness and presence of God.

Through hymn, prayer, responsive reading, and sung responses we express with our mouths what is in our hearts and our heads. Through bodily movement and active listening we take in and embody the gospel that is shared for our understanding.

Through acts of dedication we bring the performance to its denouement, as its full meaning unfolds to performers and audience. Someone once called a church office and asked, "When does the service begin?" The answer: "As soon as the worship service ends!"

Learning to Worship

We begin where all of us start—with our own experience, in our own depths. As young children, we have a natural curiosity that leads us to explore the world beyond ourselves. Long before we can give names to realities like wonder or forgiveness or grace, we have the experience. *Trusting our intuition* and developing our own natural sense of wonder, creativity, and imagination are part of learning to worship.

Part of learning to worship is *developing our attitudes* about worship. To enter the theatre of the spirit as actor is to accept some demands upon our own preparation—we are expectant that something will happen. We are open: to receive and to give. We offer ourselves, our imagination, and our energy. Two seminarians were talking one day outside a chapel, just before the service was to begin. One was hesitant about entering and pondered aloud, "I wonder who's in chapel today?"—meaning, obviously, who was the leader. The other said, "I don't know; but God will be there!" They both went in.

Part of learning to worship is *imitative*. How is it done in this place? What are the orders, forms, elements, styles, and patterns? Often it helps to enter into them, to get the feel, and then to seek explanation. It's sometimes called acting our way into a new way of being. By this we don't mean parking our brains or experience at the door. Quite the contrary. What we do mean is to learn to experience the meaning in the active mode, with all five senses at work.

People are role models for us as they lead worship or share in it. Learning by imitation doesn't mean simply copying the forms or habits of another. It means trying to get in touch with the interior world and the deep reservoirs of the spirit out of which others express their faith. We improve with practice—what Brother Lawrence called the "practice of the presence of God."

Some of our learning will come from *conversations* with neighbors and worship leaders. Why is communion celebrated in this way? Why is this or that element included? What does it mean? How did the patterns get this way—history, accident, popular request, personal preference, or denominational accent? Some learning will come from *books* or a visit to an art museum. Some will come from a reading of *the Bible*, especially the psalms and the Gospels. Much of learning to worship and to lead in worship will be *learning by doing*.

The worship of the faith community as it gathers doesn't just happen without a context. We bring to it who we are and what we've been doing. Prayers and moments of meditation each day help us to be more fully prepared for the worship event. Our attitudes of anticipation represent a crucial factor in our ability to bring to and receive from worship its fullest promise. The analogy is somewhat like a staff meeting: Although we see our colleagues day after day and in different constellations, when we come together for a staff meeting, we pull ourselves together. We are very intentional about what we're doing, what we bring, and what we expect to get out of it. The contrast between daily worship and full corporate worship is also like that.

Our convictions and our experience are important, and we will build what we do upon them. We'll stand by what works for us and for others; yet, a pattern of openness and teachableness is essential. Pastor John Robinson told the Pilgrims as they left Leyden, Holland for the New World in 1619, "God has yet more light and truth to break forth from the Holy Word." That should be our attitude also.

This Book's Approach to Worship

This approach has four elements. It sees worship as part of a *continuing tradition*. It seeks to be *wholistic*, *active/participative*, and *nonsexist*.

The pattern for the worship experience of the Christian community was set, in large measure, in the patterns of Jewish synagogue worship long before Jesus' day. Our scriptures date back from nineteen to thirty centuries. They are rooted in the experience of the people of God over multiple generations. Some hymnody, symbols, the creeds, and many prayers have been in continuing use for more than ten centuries. We carry forward the awesome experience of our forebears in the Hebrew-Christian tradition as we share or lead in worship. We value that for its rootedness and its sense of the sacred.

Yet, tradition is not a fixed, static thing. Nor is it a box in which to confine people. It is a witness to the continuity of experience. The authenticity of tradition is what it means for us now, in this moment, in this place. We enter it as heirs, continuers, and creators. New tradition will emerge from our experience and some old will atrophy. We worship a living God before whom all forms are expendable.

We seek to be wholistic in our worship. The Greek New Testament uses the same word for *whole* as it does for *holy* and for *salvation*. We want a worship experience for the whole person as well as for the whole gathered body of Christ. We are to love God with our heart, soul, mind, and strength; therefore, our patterns and forms should help us do this.

To be *active/participative* recalls the style of worship in the active mode, using all the senses. Worship is something we see, hear, touch, smell, and taste, because God meets us in our sensate life. The more completely our total being is engaged in worship, the fuller and richer will be our experience of God and our spirituality. Worship is not detached from life, for life flows from it and into it. Openness to God, to ourselves, and to neighbors in need are all part of the same participatory mode.

We seek to worship God in a *nonsexist* way. The biblical scholar Phyllis Trible speaks of the God who is above and beyond sexuality.[6] Thus, our reference to God and to persons should not be limited to the masculine or to gender-limited language. The Bible and the Christian tradition, as well as our own experience, reveal a God of truth, spirit, power, wisdom, and love. Our experience of one another and of God has sexuality dimensions as well as many other dimensions. To paraphrase a provocative title of C.S. Lewis, our God is too small if references are limited to the masculine pronoun. As this book unfolds, we will express ways in which androgynous understandings of God can take shape in our worshiping life.

Criteria for Effective Worship Leadership

The first element in preparing to lead worship is to prepare ourselves. Open up to the spirit of God. Let the Spirit's energy flow through your body and imagination. Then address such questions as, Who am I to do this act? Where am I in my self-understanding, my relationship to God and these people, my sense of the meaning of worship? Where are the people whom I or we will lead? How can their experiences and mine intersect? What is it to be onstage in the theatre of the spirit? Preparation of the self is essential.

Second, take time to think and pray your way into the situation in which you're going to be leading worship or helping others to plan worship. Prepare to answer for yourself the key newspaper reporting questions: Who? Where? How? Why? When? Like a good stew, worship should normally simmer a long time. We say normally because sometimes an occasion for worship comes up on the spur of the moment and no simmering is possible, or what we have planned no longer seems right because of changed circumstances or new information.

Third, case the joint! Your worship will take place in some space. Get the feel of it. What is it like for you and for others who will lead worship? What is it like for those who share in the service—mood, lighting, distractions, points of focus? What are the possibilities for congregational participation? What are the potential elements of movement offered by the space?

Fourth, become saturated with the theme and the key elements in worship. Use the Bible. Clip items from newspapers and magazines. Cartoons, poems, short stories, and anecdotes will help you get in touch with the theme's possibilities. Let the theme and the key elements enter fully into your inner being. Help them to become authentically you, and allow them to link you up with God and with the worshiping congregation.

Fifth, think of worship in terms of story—biography and autobiography. Sam Keen and Anne Valley Cox make the point: "To be a person is to have a story to tell. We become grounded in the present when we color in the outline of the past and the future . . . we need only claim the stories that are our birthright."[7] John Marsh contends that "every full act of Christian worship is a dramatic representation of the great themes of the Christian story."[8]

Sixth, decide where continuity in liturgy is essential and where flexibility is desirable and possible.

Seventh, be bold, creative, intentional, and tender. *Boldness* has to do with taking strong action to make the effort what you want it to be. Strong, virile elements convey your sense of purpose. People should be able to trust your sense of things and to have confidence in your leadership.

To be *creative* is to take various forms and shape them to your style, mood, and purpose. Worship should be tailored to fit the needs and style of a particular worshiping group.

To be *intentional* is to think through what you want to happen in each phase of the worship experience and to develop ways to assure its happening. For example, if you want the congregation to sing, you must answer some questions. Is music available for all? Is an accompanist available, and is she or he clear about how to begin and end? Will selections be announced? Will there be an amen? Are the people familiar with the words and tune?

Intentionality also involves what we wish to convey to others— mood, style, meaning, and timing. Rey's comments to a *Brigadoon* cast she was choreographing convey the intentionality we have in mind:

> Take five minutes to recall your position in various dances and scenes. Get clear and comfortable about where you stand. Then, think about what kind of a character you want to become—how old are you, how do you feel about that and how do you want to present yourself to the world. It's called being intentional. Let your whole body tell your story.

Tenderness is the counterpoint of boldness. Life is fragile and full of wonder. Our warmest, most caring stance honors that life and wonder. We cannot convey the caring quality of God's presence except through loving eyes, gestures, tone of voice, and spirit.

Eighth, give attention to how each element of worship can be expressed in the experience you are planning. These elements are spelled out in the next chapter.

The Rhythm of Worship. . . . Adoration, confession, acceptance, and response make worship an event in which we bring all that we are and leave refreshed and transformed by God's grace.

CHAPTER 2

The Rhythm of Worship

Deep within us is the drive to be linked up with the transcendent, awesome, and loving forces in the universe. To do this we use what we call the expressive rhythms of worship. Although they relate to elements of a worship service, they also touch dimensions of the life of any community of faith.

When planning worship keep in mind the four elements that comprise the rhythm of most worship: *adoration*—the sense of awe, wonder, and mystery; *confession*—the not-yet-ness of life and spirit; *acceptance*—the process of grace; and *response*—our offering and self-giving. Usually these elements happen in this sequence, but sometimes they appear in a different order.

These elements were conveyed in Isaiah's call twenty-five centuries ago: "In the year that King Uzziah died I saw the Lord . . . high and lifted up [6: 1]." The sense of *awe,* the *majesty* and the *wonder* of God overwhelms Isaiah. Here is *adoration!*

Isaiah's response to this awesomeness of the holy is, "Woe is me! for I am undone [Isa. 6:5, KJV]." He senses his inadequacy, sin, and incompleteness. His is an act of *confession*, of penitence. He sees himself in the mirror of the holy and of his own incompleteness and promise. The result is anger and a sense of helplessness.

A coal touches Isaiah and he hears the comforting words, "Lo, this has touched your lips and your iniquity is purged, your sin pardoned." He is *accepted*. And Isaiah accepts that gift.

Then God asks, "Whom shall I send and who will go for us?" The act of confrontation, penitence, and acceptance has not ended. Isaiah senses this and answers, "Here am I. Send me." His *response* is unwavering. His offering is complete and full.

Adoration, confession, acceptance, and response are not only themes for worship; they describe the whole life of a congregation in all its dimensions. Thus, we need to find ways to release these elements in our life together in education, evangelism, fellowship, business, and mission.

Adoration—The Sense of Awe, Wonder, and Mystery

Our worship begins with God, with our sense of the nature and the reality of the Holy One. We give God many names—Creator, Holy One, Redeemer, Amazing Grace, Mother, Father, Parent, Hope, Truth, Guiding Light, Love, and Spirit. No words can fully express the ground of our being; yet the divine reality is strongly present in our experience, as our spirits reach beyond themselves to the Great Spirit. Our loving is a reflection of the Beloved One.

Part of our celebration is gratitude. Our hearts are full of the wonderfulness of life and we give thanks. We sense human possibilities because the God who made us has put them there and meets us in the midst of problem and opportunity.

This motif of wonder is not only about God; it is also about us. We are intrigued with the capacity for self-transcendence, with our sense of awe before the universe's complexity or a sight of great beauty, or with awareness of deep love for and by another.

This opening stage of the worship experience is not a time to put it all together as in a mathematical formula, but rather to share the wonderful reach of the human spirit to the Spirit beyond. Let it soar! Let it flow free!

The word worship derives from Anglo-Saxon words meaning worth-ship. We worship one who is worthy of the highest reaches of our spirit. This mood we often call *adoration* is expressed in the ancient *Te Deum Laudamus* (the Latin means "We praise you, O God"):

> We praise thee, O God: we acknowledge thee to be the Lord.
> All the earth doth worship thee . . .
> Holy, holy, holy. Lord God of Sabaoth;
> Heaven and earth are full of the majesty of thy glory.

God doesn't need a lot of trappings to be present to us; various forms can enlarge our awareness and our sense of awe, wonder, and mystery. Sometimes great music will do this for us. Often the place of worship conveys this sense to us, and instinctively our voices are hushed. A painting, a banner, the weather, a flower arrangement, the faces of friends all transport us to that realm of the spirit we call wonder.

Rachel Carson described this sense of wonder in memorable words:

> A child's world is fresh and new and beautiful, full of wonder and excitement. It is our misfortune that for most of us that clear-eyed vision, that true instinct for what is beautiful and awe-inspiring, is dimmed and even lost before we reach adulthood. If I had influence with the good fairy who is supposed to preside over the christening of all children I should ask that her gift to each child in the world would be a sense of wonder so indestructible that it would last throughout life, as an unfailing antidote against the boredom and disenchantments of later years, the sterile preoccupation with things that are artificial, the alienation from the sources of our strength.[1]

Parts of the order of worship that relate to the adoration segment are the prelude, call to worship, introit or other choral introduction, hymn of praise or adoration, and invocation. The creed or affirmation of faith may be part of the adoration phase or it may be offered as part of the acceptance segment.

Here's a call to worship we like that imparts this sense of adoration, wonder, and personal expression:

> In the beginning there was nothing.
> Then there was light and life and a world.
> Then there was man and woman
> And they wandered in the desert.
> Then there was a people
> And a death and resurrection.
> Then there were your mother and your father.
> Then there was you.
> Let us worship God![2]

Another interesting call to worship communicates the sense of participation:

Leader: Good morning! Why are you here?
People: To celebrate God's gift of life!
Leader: This is a service of worship. It is not a performance. Will you be honest during this hour?
People: We will try to be honest.
Leader: Will your minds and hearts be open to God's word?
People: We will try to be open to God's word.
Leader: Good. Then we can proceed. Let us praise God who is Creator of all things. Who are you?
People: We are the ministers of this congregation, called by God to be servants in the world.

Leader: Why are you here?
People: We are gathered here to praise God in thought, word, prayer, and song, and to experience the fellowship of other Christians.[3]

Here is a classic prayer of adoration:

Almighty God, to you all hearts are open, all desires known, and from you no secrets are hidden. Cleanse and inform our hearts and minds by the inspiration of your Holy Spirit, that we may truly love you and worthily praise your holy Name, through Christ our Lord.[4]

Sometimes a responsive reading is part of the adoration segment. Here is a setting of Psalm 8 that is a good example both of congregational participation and the mood of adoration and wonder:

Leader: O God, how full of wonder and splendor you are.
People: I see the reflections of your beauty and hear the sounds of your majesty wherever I turn.
Leader: Even the babbling of babes and the laughter of children spell out your name in indefinable syllables.
People: When I gaze at the star-studded skies and attempt to comprehend the vast distances,
Leader: I contemplate in utter amazement my Creator's concern for me.
People: I am dumbfounded that you should care for me.
Leader: And yet you have made me in your image; you have called me your child.
People: O God, how full of wonder and splendor you are. Your name should be known in all the earth.[5]

A responsive reading should identify with the personal situation of the people as well as with the biblical faith. A Hawaiian service includes an element of thanksgiving for rainbows, one of the lovely features of Hawaiian skies:

Leader: "And God said, Behold, I establish my covenant with you and your children, and with every living creature."
People: For your covenant of faithfulness, O God, which has upheld us in the past, and for your sure promise to be with us and our children in the days ahead, we give thanks to you.
Leader: "And God said, I will establish my covenant with you; neither shall there be any more a flood to destroy the earth."
People: For this island in the sky which we call our world, and for this

island in the sea which we call our home; for the beauty and
bounty of the earth, we give thanks unto you, O holy one.

Leader: "And God said, This is the token of the covenant which I
make between me and you and every living creature, for all
generations: I do set my rainbow in the cloud, and it shall be
for a token of a covenant between me and the earth."

People: For every sign of love, in earth and sky and sea, for all the
reminders of your goodness to us which appear in sun, rain,
and rainbow, in tree, fruit, and flower, in the stars of heaven
and in the faces of our family and our friends, we give thanks.[6]

The two contemporary statements of faith that follow include various elements of the Christian story and experience. They convey the
notes of adoration and affirmation, and celebrate the sense of awe,
wonder, and mystery that are in the gospel.

We believe in God who creates and nurtures and sustains all life,
    the source of all that is,
    who has loved the whole creation throughout the ages,
    the friend and defender of the needy, the deprived, the helpless;

And we believe in Jesus of Nazareth, Jesus the Christ, redeemer and
risen Lord,
    God's gift of love for all peoples and the whole creation
    but especially for the human being: in Jesus God entered our
    world;

We believe that Jesus shows us who God is and what God intends for
the world,
    that Jesus is the way to the Creator,
    the special friend of those who do not succeed in life:
    because of Him nothing can separate us from God's love;

And we believe in the Spirit, who gives us joy in God's love for all
peoples;

We believe in the unique fellowship of those who accept God's love in
Jesus Christ—the church;

We believe that we are called by God to care for each other and the
whole earth;

We believe that in the long run life has the victory over powers of
death and that through God's love our very selves will enjoy life
everlasting.

Glory and praise to the God who brings us into full divine fellowship.

Glory and praise to Jesus Christ, gift of life eternal, clearest picture of God.

Glory and praise to that same God at work everywhere in the world through the Holy Spirit.

Our God is Good![7]

We believe in God, the Eternal Spirit, who is made known to us in Jesus our brother and to whose deeds we testify:

God calls the worlds into being, creates humankind in the divine image, and sets before us the ways of life and death.

God seeks in holy love to save all people from aimlessness and sin.

God judges all humanity and all nations by that will of righteousness declared through prophets and apostles.

In Jesus Christ, the man of Nazareth, our crucified and risen Lord,
God has come to us and shared our common lot, conquering sin and death
and reconciling the whole creation to its creator.

God bestows upon us the Holy Spirit, creating and renewing the church of Jesus Christ, binding in covenant faithful people of all ages, tongues, and races.

God calls us into the church to accept the cost and joy of discipleship,
to be servants in the service of the whole human family,
to proclaim the gospel to all the world and resist the powers of evil,
to share in Christ's baptism and eat at his table,
to join him in his passion and victory.

God promises to all who trust in the gospel forgiveness of sins and fullness of grace,
courage in the struggle for justice and peace,
the presence of the Holy Spirit in trial and rejoicing,
and eternal life in that kingdom which has no end.

Blessing and honor, glory and power be unto God. Amen.[8]

Confession—The Not-yet-ness of Life and Spirit

This sense of the not-yet calls us to shake off the old, to lay aside our sinfulness. We receive the promise of what we can be as a gift in grace. When we repent, we are forgiven. When we confess who and what we are in our vulnerability, we sense what we may become. We deal here not with false hopes, pseudoguilt, or unreachable dreams but with the heights and depths of human possibility and God's promise of what we can be now and in the days to come. Belief in human possibility is part of faith.

We stand as those naked before the Holy God, clearly revealed for who and what we are. Further, we have a sense of promise unfulfilled, for we are not yet what we can be. Our dreams and the reality of our lives do not fully mesh. The possibilities of abundant life elude us. We stand, as the scripture says, "on the tiptoe of expectation," sensing how much potential life must hold that we have yet to experience.

Our linkage with the Holy Spirit stretches us. We reach beyond the mundane and the everyday to touch the reality of God and our own spirituality. That stretching reveals the distance we have yet to go. Even as we sense the progress of our spiritual pilgrimage, we are aware of the limitations of our own spiritual response. We know our sins of commission and of omission, our incomplete fulfilling of the human promise.

In worship the sense of not-yet-ness has some personal and some corporate elements. It also has a sense of history. Individually and together we come to the moment of confession over a long time. Some of our time in the confession mode is individual—listening, examining, confronting, shedding, seeking, shaping, and yearning; some is corporate—taking in, reaching out, shaping and reshaping relationships, trying to love the unlovable, trying to be the person we want to be in community, and seeking the promise of solidarity.

Some elements of the liturgy assist us—the scripture's promise of forgiveness, the words of the confession prayer, and the assurance of pardon. Often hymn or choral settings transmit the heartbeat of confession to us.

Our prayers and patterns of confession should include the general and the specific, the corporate and the individual. The following prayer of confession is illustrative:

Holy God, you have given the earth to its creatures for the sustenance of life. You have created human beings in your image with the ability to think, plan, dream, nurture, and care. You have built in each of us the passion for community and relationship.

We confess that we have abused your gifts. We have disregarded our interdependence with our fellow passengers on this fragile space ship. We have been selfish and chosen the path to immediate gratification.

We pray for your forgiveness. Restore in us the dream of a community of caring, of pilgrims of your promise. We pray in Jesus' name. Amen.

One confession we like comes from the liturgy of the French Reformed Church:

O Lord, holy and righteous God, I acknowledge before thee that I do not fear thee and that I do not love thee above all things. I do not come to take delight in prayer nor do I continue in thy word. I lack joy in thy service. I do not have the freedom of thy children. By my distractions I waste the time which thou dost give me.

I do not really love my neighbor; I am too interested in myself. I am not always in a good mood; I am vain and susceptible. I lack the conscience that should accompany my Christian profession and the spirit of solidarity. I abuse the sufferings of others; I am not free so far as money is concerned. My heart is divided, crossed by doubts and guilty desires.

I accuse myself before thee, O God, of this mediocrity. Forgive me and fill me with the love of Jesus so that in my life something will finally be changed. Amen.

Or here is a prayer of confession that reflects a more contemporary sense of the meaning of God and the nature of our rejection of our best self as well as our not-yet-ness:

Oh God of Rachael, Leah and Ruth, God of Abraham, Isaac and Jacob: . . .

You have told us that You will be with us in the midst of change, and You have watched us cling to the false securities of consistent times, unchanging relationships and eternal beliefs.

You have asked us to love the stranger in our midst, and You have watched us ignore even the person in the same pew.

You have called us to live life to its fullest, and You have watched us deny our own potential and our own responsibility as one created in Your image.

And yet, Oh God, we are gathered here today in the belief that there is a way to overcome these fears, that we can learn to live boldly on the edge of life, that we like Ruth can follow to a new land where You have visited. For we are Your people and You are our God. So be it.[9]

Prayers of confession may relate to a particular aspect of our lives and may be specific and limited in their scope. For a worship service dealing with sexuality, the following prayer of confession was used:

> O Creator of all that we are and have, who made these miraculous bodies of ours held together by flesh and blood and sinew, we confess the misuse of your gifts. Forgive us when we have used our gender as an excuse for our failure or when we have used our sexuality to coerce and cajole another human being. Make us indignant and compassionate before any violation of human flesh, but teach us the healing power in the tender touch and loving embrace of our brothers and sisters.[10]

The segment of worship dealing with confession and penitence needs lots of silence to encourage our remembrance and review. It is a good period for choral transitions and responses by the choir. A responsive reading from the Psalms, or from contemporary literature or life emphasizes the interdependence of us all in sin and grace. Congregational singing of a prayer response or a penitent hymn gives expression to our solidarity and community. The worship leader or the congregation as a whole should share words of pardon and promise. This acknowledges our confession and our resolve and, in its own way, renews our covenant with one another and with God.

In addition to prayer and song, there are other ways to give expression to our confessions. For instance, each person can be asked to write a confession on a piece of paper and to deposit it at the altar with the money offering; or people can be asked to write on the church bulletin the names of persons with whom they wish to make their peace; or stationery can be provided for persons to take some moments during the service to drop a note to the person with whom they wish to achieve reconciliation. If the service is out of doors, the name or the act can be written on a rock and buried or thrown into a hole.

Often there seems to be a tendency to run through this section of the worship very quickly, almost as though some mystical formula would take care of the formalities. Why? Perhaps it is because we are embarrassed at the notion of confession and penitence, especially in a public context. Yet each of us knows that the confession stage is a crucial part of the rhythm of worship because of the distance between our intentions and our actions, the lure of the not-yet, and our ambivalence in the face of its demands.

We begin with a sense of wonder and awe of the divine and of persons made in the divine image; then we sense our limitations, our sins of omission and commission, and our standing on the threshold of promise. We need time to make the journey from adoration through the desert and wilderness of confession to stage three.

Acceptance—The Process of Grace

Paul Tillich wrote a book called *The Courage to Be*. His theme is that we are accepted, and the "courage to be" is the guts to accept that acceptance. Tillich has described the process of grace and acceptance in an exciting way:

> You are accepted. *You are accepted*, accepted by that which is greater than you, and the name of which you do not know. Do not ask for the name now; perhaps you will find it later. Do not try for anything now; perhaps later you will do much. Do not seek for anything; do not perform anything; do not intend anything. *Simply accept the fact that you are accepted!* If that happens we experience grace.[11]

The key motif here is wholeness, or putting things together. Acceptance has two dimensions: God's acceptance of us and our acceptance of God. This covenant is not a one-way flow of God to us; it is a mutual covenant in which God enters our experience and we are affirmed. The Christian community expresses that affirmation as it prays for all sorts and conditions of persons as a nurturing fellowship.

Sometimes, like Jacob of old, we reach for God, demanding a blessing and wrestling until one comes; and sometimes we respond immediately to God's outreach to us. In each case we accept that we are accepted. Someone put it, "I'm not O.K. and you're not O.K. and that's O.K.!" The scriptures put it this way: "We love because God first loved us." In authentic worship we experience the seeking love of God. This acceptance business is the heart, soul, and guts of the Good News. The Good News is that the creator God loves us, and that the love continues to us in Jesus Christ, in the caring community, and in the daily lives of men, women, and children. We like the way one responsive reading says it:

> We trust that beyond the absence: there is a presence.
> That beyond the pain: there can be healing.
> That beyond the brokenness: there can be wholeness.
> That beyond the anger: there may be peace.

That beyond the hurting: there may be forgiveness.
That beyond the silence: there may be the word.
That through the word: there may be understanding.
That through understanding: there is love.[12]

A variety of liturgical forms expresses this giving and sharing of acceptance—the scripture, the sermon, the ritual of friendship, the pastoral prayer, and/or prayers of intercession.

Chapter 4 describes in a fuller way the relationship of the Bible to worship. Biblical words and themes are part of the warp and woof of each element of the service. Frequently, both Old Testament and New Testament sections will be read in the same worship service. Sometimes an Old Testament reading, a Gospel reading, and an epistle reading will all be used.

In early New England worship, as, indeed, in much of the history of the church, the congregation stood for the reading of the Gospel. This reading should be a high moment for us, as the great words of faith take flesh in our lives and are conveyed through our words and inflections. Introductory explanations of the context of scripture can greatly help the congregation to get the most out of the reading. Using the Bible in pews will promote the sense of corporate reading (same version for all, please). Thoughtful, careful preparation for reading the Bible is essential. We should know how to pronounce all the words and read them with meaning. We should practice reading the words to be heard.

The craft of preaching is one that deserves the wholeness of our being. This is not a book on preaching, but some major points must be made about it. It is, in some sense, a "living out" of the scripture. Although the sermon is a highly personal statement, it is not purely autobiographical, to be sure. In fact, preaching that is largely autobiographical is generally boring; but authentic preaching reflects one's own experience even when a first-person pronoun is never used. The sermon is a communal experience even when no opportunity exists for congregational response. One preaches in the context of a continuing and caring faith community. If the intersection of lives is not reflected in that preaching, it is inauthentic.

Preaching is an art form. Its message is the passionate sharing of life. Its media are voice, gesture, and body language. Its coloration is humor, anecdote, metaphor, inflection, and perspective. Interesting subject matter and a good sense of timing are essential. Like any craft, good preaching is the result of skill and practice. In a fundamental sense the medium is the message—body, voice, and eye language convey what we mean even when the words are different.

On the negative side, the sermon is a one-way medium which creates a communication problem that must be taken seriously. Good use of the medium helps enormously. It can be made to seem more dialogical, even when it is not, by using questions, anecdotes, and metaphors that draw strong response from the congregation. Dialogue sermons are a way of modifying the medium. A talk-back session or a suggestion box can help. Visual aids can enhance the oral character of the preaching medium.

Much that has been said about the sermon applies also to meditations, although the latter are usually briefer and often focus on a single theme. Because awe, confession, and response are part of the medium and the message, the subject matter of sermon or meditation does not concentrate solely upon the acceptance element of the four-fold rhythm; but in a special way the sermon or meditation will play out the acceptance covenant of God and the people.

For many Christian traditions the communion or eucharist is the climax and focal point of the liturgy. A number of Reformed congregations are recovering the dual emphases of preaching and the Lord's Supper, word and table. Oftentimes, even when communion is not part of the worship service, its importance is still emphasized at some point. We have chosen to discuss communion later in this chapter, as it relates to the response section of the worship service. It constitutes God's response to men and women and invites our response in return.

If the sacrament is celebrated as the sole focus of the liturgy, the four elements are included in a natural way. We stand in awe of God's presence as we focus on the bread and the wine, which are symbolic of Jesus' sacrifice and promise. We are called upon to make peace with one another as we confess our unworthiness. By taking the bread and the cup we accept our acceptance so that we may enter into a new covenant of intention and promise.

Response—Our Offering and Self-giving

It is not enough to say, "I accept," although acceptance is the first step. Our response must take concrete form. There is no cheap grace here. Discipleship has both a cost and a joy. The response we make to the other three elements—adoration, confession, and acceptance—and to meeting God in our midst takes many forms. Sometimes we quietly celebrate being at one with God and with our own possibilities. Jesus' action on the cross symbolizes this. The act is called atonement, as in at-one-ment. Sometimes our response is a new commitment to action or mission. We discover new possibilities for our lives and resolve to make them happen. It has to do with being a good neighbor and sharing the good news with others. Sometimes our response is a continuing struggle of the soul for light and direction. Although we sense our forgiveness and acceptance by God, the struggles of our lives are too intense for us to move easily into the response phase, so we continue to wrestle and struggle because that is the best response we can make for the time.

Our liturgy needs to provide for these diverse responses. One church has a candle of life in the chancel, which it lights for particular passages or new events—birth, death, confirmation, church membership, graduation, recovery from illness or surgery. Another church selects a different person each Sunday to share what the life of the church means to him or her. Many churches use a ritual of friendship in which everyone signs a guest register and each person greets neighbors in the pew.

Sharing the concerns of the congregation can be a vibrant part of the service. This happens just before or after the pastoral prayer or the offering. Persons share, orally, an issue, a person, a prayer concern, an announcement, or an event whose happening impacts the life of the congregation. Response is made by the worship leader and in pastoral or intercessory prayers.

We have already examined the role of Holy Communion as God's response. This offering, this self-giving calls forth a response from us. The offering is one worship element through which our response in faith and dedication is made. Sometimes two offerings take place—the first is the bringing forth of the communion elements; the second—which often follows the taking of the elements—is our response in kind.

The sacrament of Holy Communion begins the offering. The rite includes the invitation, the breaking of bread and the giving of wine, the distribution of the elements, and a prayer of thanksgiving. A fuller treatment of communion is included in the next chapter and in the Appendix.

Stewardship involves giving time, talent, and treasure. Giving is in the active mode; thus, it is important that churches think of ways in which each of these dimensions can be reflected in the offering. For example, in most churches people sit in the pew, waiting for the collection to be taken. In contrast, churches that want the offering to be in the active mode ask each person to place her or his gift on the altar. If there is a difficulty due to numbers or the time it takes, ushers are stationed throughout the sanctuary so people can move to a nearby offering plate. The main thing is to "do it," rather than wait for it. Thus, we bodily express our dedication and promise to God and self, a prelude to acts of commitment that follow.

One prayer of dedication for the offering uses these words:

> Accept these offerings of money, O God. They are given by many persons for different purposes. Use both the persons and the reason to your glory. Teach us how to give as receivers of grace. In Christ's name. Amen.[13]

At the close of the service and to end the response phase, a hymn of dedication is appropriate. Usually it is in four-four time, to convey a moving out.

A benediction (literally "the good word") is a gathering up and a sending forth. Many times it is biblical. One benediction we like is:

> O God, take our minds and think through them,
> Take our lips and speak through them,
> Take our hearts and set them on fire. Amen.[14]

Quite often a response to the benediction is made by the choir; this can be effective and appropriate. Many congregations sing a response to the benediction. For example, either the spiritual "Amen" or the words to the hymn "God Be with You 'Til We Meet Again" could be used for a benediction response. Sometimes the service is concluded by the forming of a friendship circle.

The postlude is not cover music or an addendum; it is a form of offering and dedication. Some congregations remain seated or standing in place during the postlude, as the organ or the instrumentalist expresses musically the motif of offering, response, and gift.

Our attitude as we leave the church tells a lot about the character of our response. Do we manifest joy, dedication, elation, expectation, and a sense of mission? Do we greet our neighbor gladly and with empathy? Do we leave with a sense of solidarity, enabled in part through the love energies we release toward others? As we answer these questions we express the nature of our response.

Most worship services include the four elements discussed in this chapter and the rhythmic movement from one to the next. Sometimes our worship will focus more on one element than another, but when this happens we miss some of the completeness of the worship cycle to which our spirits are geared.

Worship is an event that is expressive of the deepest elements in our individual and corporate experiencing—adoration, confession, acceptance, and response. We bring to it all that we have and are, and through some mysterious processes of grace we are transformed by it. We are renewed and our world is made new. We understand afresh God's calling to love our neighbors and to pursue ministries of compassion and of justice. It is a big deal, worthy of our best imagination and dedication!

Faith and Form. . . . As we express our faith in prayer, let us lift our eyes, heads, and arms so as to receive forgiveness and reach out for new energy and possibilities.

CHAPTER 3

Faith and Form

This chapter focuses on prayer and faith, and their forms of expression. It touches the heart and soul of the believer in the midst of our searching and relationships. It is about the patterns of our lives in our solitude and in our community.

Prayer

Margaret Mead was in the midst of an animated conversation with colleagues about energy, social justice, and ecology when the tape recorder caught her words as the mood shifted: "Prayer does not use up any artificial energy, it doesn't burn up any fossil fuel, it doesn't pollute. Neither does song, neither does love, neither does the dance."[1]

In our approach to faith and form we begin with prayer—conversation with God, the linking of heart with heart, the web of human connectedness. Often we think we don't pray but, in fact, we do it all the time. We do reach beyond ourselves when we are elated or when we are struck by despair. Everyone practices some form of prayer. Marks on ancient caves as well as a gasped, "Oh, my God!" testify to this connectedness of us humans with the forces beyond ourselves.

Part of the glue that holds the Bible's diverse pieces together is the personal communication of persons with God. Beginning with the conversations in the garden of the first woman and man and continuing through the visions of Revelation, the Bible is a book of prayer. The Bible reflects various types of prayer: for instance, Isaiah 6:5 and Psalm 27:7-14 are prayers of confession; Psalm 63:1-8 is a prayer of praise; and Jesus' agony in the garden, reflected in John 17:1-26, is a prayer of intercession.

Because prayer was central in Jesus' life, one of the most vivid New Testament pictures is of his slipping away from the disciples or the crowds for periods of prayer. Jesus did this to stress the im-

27

portance of each person doing her or his own prayer without show or fanfare.

In Matthew 6:5-15 Jesus shared with us his own prayer, the Lord's Prayer, which is the best known Christian prayer. Because it has been thought of as the Christian's devotional model, it is important that we look at its form and content. Notice that God is addressed personally, and then God is praised. Note also that the prayer uses "us," the first-person plural form, so that the individual is not lost but is set in a corporate context.

In the Lord's Prayer we—
    confess our hope in the coming of God's realm;
    link ourselves with God's will;
    pray for daily sustenance;
    seek forgiveness and to be forgiving;
    and pray for deliverance.
The final phrase—"the kingdom and the power and the glory"—was added by the church some generations after the New Testament was written. Like any good doxology, it is a fitting close.

The fact this phrase was added later is a reminder that the life of worship is a developing one. Interestingly, Roman Catholics say the Lord's Prayer without including this last phrase. Many Protestants think Catholics are more strongly oriented to tradition than they; yet it is the Catholics, in this instance, who are more scriptural in their Lord's Prayer form.

We can prevent this prayer from becoming the "vain repetitions" Jesus warns us about in Matthew 6:7 (KJV) by using different versions from time to time. This helps us to get back to the root meanings of various phrases and petitions and to avoid the sexism used in some versions.

The Revised Standard Version translation of Matthew 6:9-13 follows:

> Our Father who art in heaven,
> Hallowed be thy name.
> Thy kingdom come,
> Thy will be done,
>   On earth as it is in heaven.
> Give us this day our daily bread;
> And forgive us our debts,
>   As we also have forgiven our debtors;
> And lead us not into temptation,
>   But deliver us from evil.

The Lord's Prayer is also found in what may be an earlier version in Luke 11:1-4. Here is another version of the prayer, which we also like:

> Our God in heaven,
>   holy be your name,
>   your kingdom come,
>   your will be done
>   on earth as in heaven.
> Give us today the bread we need.
> Forgive us our sins
>   as we forgive
>   those who sin against us.
> Save us in the time of trial.
>   and deliver us from evil.
> For the kingdom, the power, and the glory
>   are yours now and forever.
> Amen.[2]

Prayer itself is a discipline and an art; therefore, one who would lead prayer must be a person of prayer. If one has not done much praying, a season with the psalms is a good place to start. Keep a notebook or 3 × 5 cards handy in order to note passages that have important meaning and to write prayer phrases of your own. Devotional classics such as Dag Hammarskjöld's *Markings*, E. Stanley Jones' *The Way*, Thomas R. Kelly's *A Testament of Devotion*, or *The Daily Word* can nurture the prayer life.[3]

Each day set aside a period for quiet meditation and prayer in order to build a discipline. Discipline helps us make prayer a continuing reality in our life whether we're in the mood or not. It is akin to dancers going to dance classes even after they have jobs. Our life stays even when we use prayer as a continuing discipline and resource.

Charles Francis Whiston suggests thinking of prayer as snow-flakes—each one is a little different.[4] Each is beautiful in its own way, and although small, when piled up together they make a substantial covering for our faith existence. This idea of snowflake prayers can enrich our worship, so try offering a snowflake prayer!

These efforts to be persons of prayer and to enable the congregation to become a prayer community are directed toward the energies at the center of the universe. God is active in the world, and prayer is a way of being in touch with that activity. The people of God are a people of contemplation and of action, through which the energies of caring are released. Our corporate praying, when we are together and when we are scattered, builds a strong force for support and action.

Corporate prayers are in different modes and moods. There are prayers of adoration, confession, intercession, thanksgiving, dedication, and benediction.

Prayers of *adoration* are directed to God and affirm the winsomeness of the Holy One. They are used at the beginning of a worship service. Psalm 145:1-3 is an excellent example:

> I will extol thee, my God and King,
>   and bless thy name for ever and ever.
> Every day I will bless thee,
>   and praise thy name for ever and ever.
> Great is the Lord, and greatly to be praised,
>   and [God's] greatness is unsearchable.

A prayer of *confession* usually contains four elements: a recognition of God's and our intentions; a sense of corporate sinning; a sense of individual betrayal and action; and a prayer for forgiveness and restoration to community. For example:

> Holy God, you have called us to use our gifts for the care of the earth and the love of our neighbors. We are part of a hedonous, selfish, covetous, and greedy generation—abusing the earth and damning our neighbors. Both by my silence and my actions I participate in this sinful scheme. I pray for forgiveness for the abuse of your promise in me. Restore me and each of us to a true community of compassion, caring, and justice. Through Jesus Christ, our Lord. Amen.

Prayers of *intercession* are offered on behalf of someone else. We use them to intercede for another. Such prayers are usually intended for groups or classes of petitioners (those who face sorrow this day) or for specific happenings and concerns (peace in the Middle East or the settling of a strike). We often pray by name for those facing specific dilemmas (Mary Jane, who is facing an operation, or our high school seniors as they face an uncertain future with all its risks and opportunities). Charles Francis Whiston suggests an imaginative way to use the Lord's Prayer as a means of intercession:

> Our heavenly Father:
>   Thy name be hallowed in Richard,
>   Thy kingdom come in him,
>   Thy will be done in him today,
>   As it is in heaven.[5]

Prayers of *thanksgiving* express gratitude for a single thing: a peace treaty, the receding of floodwater, a couple united in marriage, or recovery from illness. They may include a group of petitions for both specific and general things. Many of Paul's letters open with thanksgiving prayers. However, 1 Corinthians 1:4-9 and Philippians 1:3-11, for example, would need to be adapted if they were used as worship resources. Here is a thanksgiving prayer:

> We give thanks, O holy God, for your ministries of health and healing first expressed in Jesus and in Luke, the beloved physician. For the health-giving quality of the life of our congregation, we give you thanks. Receive our searching for health of body, mind, and spirit, and make us vessels of your health-giving grace, through Jesus Christ, our Lord. Amen.

A prayer of *dedication* comes in the response section of a worship service. It should reflect both the individual and the corporate note of dedication in response to God's actions. Francis of Assisi's prayer, while cast in the individual mode, is a classic prayer of dedication.:

> O Lord, our Christ, may we have thy mind and thy spirit; make us instruments of Thy peace; where there is hatred, let us sow love; where there is injury, pardon; where there is discord, union; where there is doubt, faith; where there is despair, hope; where there is darkness, light; and where there is sadness, joy.
>
> O divine Master, grant that we may not so much seek to be consoled as to console; to be understood, as to understand; to be loved, as to love; for it is in giving that we receive, it is in pardoning that we are pardoned, and it is in dying that we are born to eternal life. Amen.

A prayer of *benediction* is like a charge, the final empowerment in a worship service. Here is an illustration from Philippians 4:23: "The grace of the Lord Jesus Christ be with your spirit."

In our worship planning we need to foster both individual and corporate praying, including that of the worship leaders. Our planning should also give attention to the ways praying together will strengthen the prayer life of our congregation. Will our prayers make contact with the experience of the people? Are there images suggested that people can take with them through the week? Have we enhanced the discipline and the art of praying? Is there enough time and a nurturing atmosphere for silent prayer?

Those responsible for the life of worship in a congregation need to give special consideration to the forms of prayer. Silent prayer deserves specific planning. Frequently, people are embarrassed by silence. They may not know what is expected of them or what to do. Therefore, worship leaders need to be clear about purposes and expectations. How does silent prayer fit in with the total flow of worship? How long will the silent period last? What guidance will be given to the worshipers about what to pray for or how? Individuals and congregations can gain skill in praying silently; this is one of the disciplines of the prayer life.

The worship bulletin can offer sample sentences or phrases to pray or contemplate. It can also suggest people or causes for whom to pray.

In addition to including prayer as an element in worship services, consider prayer groups, a prayer chain, prayer vigils, and a prayer list. *Prayer groups* can be organized around different centers— among businesspeople; a breakfast group; a daytime or evening pattern; a youth or women's group; or a group focusing on a particular concern, such as world peace or hunger. Intentionality is crucial. Persons should be asked to commit themselves for a specified period of time. The discipline of the group, in part, is to stay together beyond the first blush that brought them together. It is the motif of Matthew 18:20—"where two or three are gathered in my name."

A *prayer chain* is a group of people, each of whom agrees to pray for another in the group. The result is that each person has someone praying for him or her, and each person is praying for someone.

In a *prayer vigil* individuals sign up to pray for a particular period of time, such as New Year's Eve or Maundy Thursday night. A vigil may also be offered on behalf of an individual facing a crisis. Although vigils are often kept in sanctuaries, they may be spent in homes or at work places as well.

A *prayer list* is a list of persons toward whom prayer is to be directed over a period of time. Many times these names are printed in the worship bulletin or the church newsletter, and the whole congregation is urged to remember them in prayers. A variation is to pray in public for a group of people (mothers on Mother's Day, persons graduating from high school, church school teachers, or town leaders facing a crucial decision).

Our efforts at becoming a community of prayer should be highly intentional and disciplined. No one should be left out because of age or handicaps or difficulties with transportation or language. "The church that prays together stays together." After all, the prayer life of the church is the energy at the core of its being.

Frequently, we seem embarrassed about prayer or our efforts to become a community of prayer. The congregation needs to work at not being embarrassed by its prayer life. This effort to be a praying body is at the very heart of our faith empowerment as a people.

Faith

Faith is not a fixed condition of human experience. "I believe; help my unbelief!" the father of the sick child cried (Mark 9:24). This cry rings true to our experience in that we *do* believe but continue to reach for evidence. We build together toward the future on the past's track record. For instance, we expect the sun to rise tomorrow because it rose yesterday and today. We expect God to be present and fruitful because our experience leads to that conviction. Although there is an interrelatedness of seeing and believing, we see because we believe rather than the other way around.

Both the Greeks and the Romans had essential words to describe faith. The Greek *credo* means "I believe." We speak of a credo as a personal statement of convictions. That is an important meaning of faith.

A second meaning is expressed in the Latin word *assensus*, to give "assent." We place our signature on a document to note our assent to a proposition or a course of action we believe will happen. To give assent is an act of will, as we affirm a set of propositions or the validity of a statement.

Perhaps the most profound meaning of faith is conveyed in the Latin word *fiducia*, which means "trust." Faith, at its heart, is a relationship of trust between persons—or between persons and God. The word fidelity comes from this root.

All three meanings—credo, assent, and trust—are involved in our experience of God. As the struggling swimmer learns to trust the water's buoyancy, so the person of faith finds a trustworthy core in human experience. Tillich spoke of God as the Ground of our Being, the sense of undergirding solidness. The Bible uses metaphors of fatherhood and motherhood to convey this sense of faithful rootedness.[6] When we speak of God as love, it is important to remember that at the heart of all loving is not only caring but trust.

We express our faith in a variety of forms. Robert Bellah contends that religion is "a set of symbolic forms and acts that relate . . . [us] to the ultimate conditions of . . . existence."[7] Faith's forms are *symbol, language, rite, ritual, myth, sacrament,* and *creed.*

A *symbol* is something that stands for or represents another thing. It has power in itself to evoke response as people identify with its meaning statement. A symbol may be an object, but it could also be a word or a phrase. We will deal with symbols in the next chapter. In fact, *language* is also a symbolic form. Certain sounds and written marks consistently represent another something. Members of a given language community agree that a certain sound or mark has a particular meaning.

A *rite* is a pattern or act that embraces a set of meanings. We speak of the rite of confirmation, which involves a declaration of faith and the commissioning of a person for full participation in the church's life. A rite may be using a rose to symbolize the birth of a child, or it may be a pattern of lighting or extinguishing the candles. A *ritual* is a set form or system of rites. Ritual is, as Evelyn Underhill reminds us, "an agreed pattern of ceremonial movements, sounds, and verbal formulas creating a framework within which corporate religious action can take place."[8] See the Appendix for illustrations of corporate worship rituals.

Webster defines *myth* as a "traditional story of unknown authorship ostensibly with an historical base but serving usually to explain some phenomenon of nature, the origin of humanity, or the customs, institutions, or religious rites of a people."[9] To speak of a thing as a myth does not mean that it is untrue. Instead, it is a literary form that is a poetic expression rather than a prose form of truth. Thus, the Adam and Eve story and the Jonah story are myths. They convey universal truths of human experience because a culture has placed great meaning in them.

A *sacrament* is a symbolic act that is rooted in scripture and tradition. In the case of the universally accepted sacraments—baptism and communion—they are rooted in Jesus' own experience. He legitimates the sacrament. The classic definition of sacrament is "an outward and visible sign of an inward and spiritual grace."

A *creed* is a formal statement of belief usually prepared for congregational rather than individual use. An individual may write a credo, but those liturgical elements we call creeds have corporate and historic grounding. Statements of faith function in congregational worship much the same as creeds do.

It is important to envision symbols and symbolic acts in the active mode. They are not things in the sense of being fixed or totally settled in meaning. Liturgical elements must convey faith in an active way as they represent persons searching for one another and for God, and as emblems of our trusting. Therefore, faith and form interact; they are interdependent. We choose symbolic forms to express our faith. These forms and those created by others address us, and often we make a faith response to them, because symbols do not remain vital apart from faith's response. Without faith they become relics or museum pieces.

Language

In the hymn "O Sacred Head, Now Wounded" the question is asked, "What language shall I borrow to thank thee, dearest friend?" Language is a resource we "borrow" or create to express faith. Language is not *the* reality; it is only a form by which we communicate meaning and experience.

Language patterns have a certain arbitrariness about them. The number or shape of the letters bears no special relationship to the reality they symbolize. Caterpillar is a big word for a small creature. Conversely, some of the largest realities in our experience—ape, lion, air, fire, earth, ocean, water, sky, sun, rain, wind—have few letters. Language is symbolic not representational.

Language evolves over time. It changes as time changes in order to be a more precise instrument of human communication and meaning. Some words retain their meaning over long periods of time; others shift their meaning somewhat quickly. Then there are new words, which belong to the growing edge of linguistic expression.

Although experience and language are interdependent, experience generally precedes language; we find the word to convey what we have experienced. Such language becomes symbolic, and those outside the experience must enter into both the experience and the symbol in order to understand the meaning of the words. Take the word love, for example. The New Testament uses three different Greek words to symbolize love—erotic love, sisterly or brotherly love, and divine love. Our English word love cannot begin to differentiate those meanings, let alone today's patterns of loving relationships. Behind the word love is our experience of love. To communicate we must work at finding word symbols which represent our experience and touch that of others in common ways.

Religious language is a mixture of long-term tradition and of contemporary new forms of experience; however, all religious language, old or new, is symbolic in form. There is no universal language of religion. Each language community uses its own forms to convey such common experiencings as God, holy, love, sin, and forgiveness. Language is learned. It continues to evolve. Some words must be changed. For example, the King James Version of the Bible uses the word suffer to translate the word Jesus uses to plead for the free response of children to him. Another illustration relates to 1 Corinthians 13. At the time the King James Version was authorized, "charity" meant self-giving, concerned love. Today it conjures up visions of self-pity and of handouts to the poor.

Humans are tool-using animals, and language is our most distinguishing tool. We sometimes say that "actions speak louder than words," but that notion can be deceptive. Obviously, words without meaning are a sham. But we live in a culture in which language is highly developed and where being able to read and to communicate orally are essential skills. However well developed our actions are (and in the church we talk a better game than we play), getting our language straight is crucial. Regrettably, our action vocabulary is severely limited, and thus our words are more crucial in themselves and as energizers of our actions.

As we said earlier, any group of people develops a language of its own. This has the effect of excluding others. Therefore, when a congregation creates and uses language, it needs to be sure such language both reflects the community as it currently is and has the room to include others. For instance, the word salvation is a central biblical concept. Essentially, it means to be whole. Unfortunately, it has become a word of judgment in the form of the question, "Are you saved?" or as an elitist expression when Christians are encouraged to do business only with born-again Christians. This is a good example of a word that has lost its precision and has to be explained before any common understanding can be achieved.

A congregation needs to be self-conscious about building a vocabulary. We want to be fully in the Hebrew-Christian tradition, and being intentional involves exploring the depth, diversity, and richness of that tradition. We also want to be contemporary and relevant. We want what we say to represent the nature of our experience and to be meaning-full language for all members of our faith community. We want language to symbolize our faith. Part of being intentional involves discovering word metaphors that connect with our experience. We want to meet the God "who makes all things new," and our intentionality involves finding language that reaches beyond our present experience. The hymn "God of Concrete, God of Steel" and metaphors about galaxies and an expanding universe reflect this notion.

A good place to begin in being intentional about vocabulary is with God language. We need language that is true to the Bible and that draws us beyond ourselves into the richness of the meaning of God in human experience. We tend to confine our God words to Lord, King, and Father. The first two represent an ancient and medieval rulership. "Father" defines a particular familial setting. All three are male-oriented. The Bible uses dozens of words to describe God; the majority of them have no reference to feudal patterns or to gender. A sampling includes Creator, Liberator, Maker, Defender, Friend, Rock, Eternal One, Holy One, Spirit, Wisdom, Love, Power, and Mercy.

Krister Stendahl, a New Testament scholar and former dean of Harvard Divinity School, says that

> the masculinity of God, and of God-language is a cultural and linguistic accident, and I think one should also argue that the masculinity of the Christ is of the same order. To be sure, Jesus Christ was a male, but that may be no more significant to his being than the fact that presumably his eyes were brown.[10]

All language about God is limiting and an approximation; therefore, we must try to use diverse metaphors such as holy, love, goodness, truth, beauty, power, parent, father, mother, creator, eternal one, and wisdom. Yet we know God is more than these metaphors. As in all ages, we need openness to new understandings and more contemporary ways to express the divine reality.

Language that attributes to God or to persons the characteristics of only one gender is troubling for two reasons: First, although basic words that described people and God were often translated in the masculine form, the Hebrew and the Greek of the Bible do not limit themselves to this form. Feminine and androgynous metaphors for God abound in both testaments. Therefore, our translations should represent the fullness of the biblical view rather than shrink it into our modern masculine mold. Second, such usage limits our representation of God or of humanity to the characteristics we understand to be acceptable for the chosen gender. God then becomes our stereotype.

Because we get comfortable with language and it is easy to take it for granted, we easily settle into our pet words and buzz phrases that we do not like to have challenged. In a fundamental sense our words are us. Yet from time to time our words need to change in order to reflect the changing people we are. We need to be encouraged to see that the challenge of creating new language expressions is not an affront to our integrity but an opportunity to create forms that communicate. Words are only symbols. They are meant to be windows through which we see reality. If they become opaque, they need cleaning, and if they no longer offer an adequate view, they need to be replaced.

Rey reflected upon the issue of language in a piece entitled "Why All the Fuss About Language?" It goes like this:

I want to share some very personal feelings. I became part of the Women's Movement because I am concerned about how difficult it is for women to get credit, about the widening pay gap between the sexes, about the dashed hopes of women who sought professional careers, and about the small number of visible women in our political, economic, and religious life. But the one thing I did not understand was the concern about language: words such as "chairman," "God the Father," "mankind." Why all the fuss? It was just picky when there were bigger, more pressing issues at hand. I'm sure many of you feel that way as you hear speakers struggle awkwardly to demasculinize their language.

Today, I'm in a different place. Let me share my journey with you. Tucked away in an issue of *Redbook* magazine, I found a short story of a 3½-year-old girl who was watching "Sesame Street." Instructions for some activity were being given by the instructor to the children, and masculine pronouns were used: "First he does this; then he does that." The little girl turned off the television set in tears because she was not included and she wanted to participate. I was struck by how easily we adults intellectualize about the generic nature of masculine words, but not that little girl—she was experiencing being unincluded, a non-person.

My next step: I figured if all these masculine words were really generic, it would be no big deal to use the feminine and that would also be generic. But that didn't happen! Use woman to include man—say Mr. Elizabeth Jernigan rather than Mrs. Fred Register—say she and leave out he—and it just doesn't sound right and passions rise. And when passions rise, people are invested; it is important. That said to me that things were not just casually generic. Chairman, postman, milkman—these words meant men because men held those jobs. And physicians' textbooks read "he" because they mean *he*, and nurses' text say "she" because they mean *she*.

I began to look further and discovered the language game played by biblical translators. In the New Testament, masculine nouns and pronouns have often been substituted for the nouns and pronouns of common gender in the original Greek. Thus, in John 1:12 and 1 John 3:1 (KJV), we read that Jesus gives us the power to become the sons of God, whereas the Greek clearly states "children" of God. In many instances, "no man" and "any man" are used instead of "no one" or "any one." For instance in 1 Timothy 3:5, "If a man knows not how to rule his own house," rather than "If any one know not. . . ." Similarly in 1 Timothy 3:1, "If a man aspires to the office of bishop . . ." rather than "if any one aspires."

Elohim, one of the many words for God in the Old Testament, is a feminine plural form. It is the plural of *Elah*, a feminine God, *not* of *El*, a masculine God. However, a masculine word ending ("im") is used, so in essence God is both male and female, which is in keeping with the androgynous god of that historical period. Note that Elohim is always translated *He*. The Holy Spirit is one of those feminine persons translated "he" in the New Testament. Yet the Hebrew word for spirit is feminine and the Greek word for spirit is neuter.

One last biblical story—about Phoebe. Paul says she was a "diakonos," in Romans 16:1, a word that is nearly always translated "minister." Then he calls her "prostatis," in Romans 16:2, meaning ruler. Yet in the King James Version, minister is changed to "servant" in reference to Phoebe, the only time "diakonos" is so translated in the entire New Testament. If you read the Revised Standard Version, she is a "deaconess" even though there were no deaconesses in New Testament times, when both women and men held the office of deacon. In fact, Greek has a separate word for deaconess which isn't used in the Bible. Therefore, Romans 16:1 reads, "I commend you to our sister Phoebe, a deaconess of the church at Cenchreae, that you may . . . help her in whatever she may require from you, for she has been a helper of many and of myself as well." In fact, it should read, "I commend you to our sister Phoebe, a minister of the church at Cenchreae, that you may help her in whatever she may require from you, for she has been a ruler of many and of myself as well." Hardly sounds the same! Please understand that I am not a biblical scholar, but I can read what scholars have written, and it has been an enlightening experience.

Then I ran into a study reported in *Human Behavior*. Over a period of time, letters were sent to people in the counseling profession. They were first asked to describe a healthy male personality; some time later, to describe a healthy female personality; later again, a healthy personality. With few exceptions, the healthy male personality and the healthy personality coincided. I found that to be personally devastating.

As a result, I have become concerned about the subtle traps language sets up for us—our dreams and expectations, our stereotypes and visual images. The Blacks have taught us that: Blacks instead of niggers, women instead of broads; from eating watermelon to women drivers, from lazy and shiftless to silly and dumb.

Language not only expresses ideas and concepts, but—I think—it may actually *shape* them. Often the process is unconscious, yet I feel the role of language is so powerful in its imprint upon the human mind that even the violated group may begin to accept the very expressions that aid in its stereotyping. Thus to change them seems picky and unimportant. I would like to affirm our struggle with language and all its awkwardness. I have come to appreciate deeply the word and concept "humanity," and I hope you will too.

Language in a society doesn't develop apart from that society's historical, economic, and political evolution. Men really have been the most remembered people in history—the economic and political movers. Yet language is the mirror reflecting society's attitudes and thinking. As a society changes (and we see this in the increasing role of women in the United Church of Christ), in its concepts through political action and education, its language patterns must be modified to be an accurate mirror. I hope you can appreciate my journey—and that it has been helpful to your journey.[11]

Ed chaired the Joint Educational Development task force, which was formed to develop guidelines to avoid stereotypes about persons and sexist language about God. He interpreted this concern by asking,

What's in a word? An image? They are our attempts to share the pictures in our heads, to convey meaning to one another. Words are noises we make or marks we put on paper by which we convey and perceive what reality is. Powerful stuff, these symbols of what is and what may be.

The JED partner denominations have a long and deep concern about symbols of meaning. We want our symbols to express the fullest meanings of God and humanity and to convey a world of mutuality without stereotypes. Our concern has taken the form of guidelines for program planners, writers, editors, artists, and leaders. We mean them to apply to the visual, printed, and spoken word.

We intend to avoid ageist, sexist, and racist stereotypes and to transcend narrow nationalism. We intend to portray the diversity and uniqueness of all ages, racial and ethnic groups, women and men, single persons, familial situations, and exceptional persons with special learning needs. Our vision of a common humanity honors difference without caricature.

The achievement of these objectives has several dimensions—*positive, negative, explicit, implicit*. It is important to convey in *positive* terms the meanings we intend: Clergy are both women and men. The hues of humanity are black, brown, red, white, and yellow. The church is inclusively intergenerational. *Negative* images are to be avoided: facial characteristics which stereotype, portrayals of women as weak and dependent or of men as without emotion and compassion.

Some of our word and graphic images are *explicit* with regard to affirmative action. We want people to meet both the women and the men of the Bible, to learn about the experiences of Hispanic or Korean or Native American persons, to discover that black is beautiful, to meet blondes and brunettes and redheads. These efforts to use explicit images are usually effective as long as they are not contrived.

It is the *implicit* which spells trouble: We portray workers and they are all male or gender typecast. We show a church sanctuary photograph intended to be universal but dominated by an American flag. We portray Jesus' calling to faith and stereotype Pharisees.

God language is particularly problematical. Our feelings and experience in this area are intense. The Old Testament people thought God so awesome that all word symbols were risky. Patriarchal though they were, they refused to use exclusively masculine pronouns for God. Sometimes they used the feminine. Often they used nongender words such as spirit, word, truth, and life. All word symbols for God are approximations. Hence, the JED guidelines ask for equal time for female, male, androgynous, and nongender metaphors for God.[12]

Rites and Rituals

A *rite* is a single ceremonial act or form. It may be part of a larger ritual. Two examples are the offering pattern and the rite of confirmation. Or—as in the case of extreme unction, or last rites—it may be self-contained. A rite has a persistent shape and flow.

Every culture has some form of rites of passage, those celebrations of the transitional in human experience. Gwen Kennedy Neville describes three elements in each such rite—separation, transition, and incorporation.[13] In the *separation* stage a person "moves out" from the situation that is being left. The *transition* phase is often the longest and constitutes the in-between stage, when one is neither fish nor fowl. The individual has left but has not yet arrived. Ambiguity and ambivalence characterize this period. In the *incorporation* phase a person begins to settle into her or his new status, sharing the life of the new community and taking on the trappings of that status.

Baptism, confirmation, marriage, ordination, and rites of burial are all rites of passage. Many churches develop intentional rites related to persons graduating from high school, moving to a new town, or entering into a new household. Each of these rites needs to include the three components Neville describes.

A rite of passage recognizes that something special is happening to a person and that he or she will never be the same again. Although the new phase may prove to be only temporary, the stage being left will be part of history and of past identity. A rite of passage also means substantial change for loved ones and others in the community of belonging, for as the person changes so does the community of persons who are related to him or her. Therefore, rites are community affairs because all are affected.

Confirmation rites illustrate these characteristics of a rite of passage. It is a once-and-for-all happening and therefore it is a watershed event. Decisions are made, vows are taken, and public intentions are declared that will always be part of one's history and identity. The confirmand's changed status affects other family members, who understand the rite as confirming elements of adulthood and self-expression. The rite is celebrated in the midst of the whole community of faith, and all join in at certain points. The laying on of hands represents the link with the church through the ages. In the Anglican and the Catholic traditions the bishop does the confirming and symbolizes the whole church's presence in this occasion.

In the Christian funeral a variety of elements are present. We celebrate the person who has died. Body and spirit are commended to God's care. The event symbolizes that the world has changed for all the persons involved. The community senses the fragility of life and its transitoriness even as it draws upon faith and memory to find meaning in the midst of grief and in the sense of separation and loss. Guilt, anger, brokenness are widely shared among the gathered community. The rite, as it employs the richness of the Christian word and tradition, gives expression to each of these meanings.

Ritual is a consistent pattern by which the elements of worship are given order and form. There are patterns of language and ceremony, movement and response. Dom Gregory Dix speaks of it as "the shape of the liturgy."[14] We might also speak of it as the vertebrate structure. Faith, of course, is prior to form, and the form embodies faith's dimensions and flow.

Rite and ritual are persistent necessities for human coping with the facts of life. Anthropologist Benson Saler describes the experience of our early ancestors with such forms:

> All of the available evidence suggests that religious rituals have a long history on earth. Neanderthal Man, who lived perhaps 50,000 to 100,000 years ago, apparently engaged in religious activities. [The dead were buried] . . . near the mouths of caves in a highly stylized way, and the archaeological evidence points to mortuary rituals. This is even more clearly the case where Cro-Magnon Man is concerned. . . . [The bodies of dead persons were decorated] . . . with a colored clay. . . . But perhaps the most dramatic examples of ancient . . . religiosity are provided by the famous Old Stone Age cave paintings of Western Europe. These paintings depict game animals, hunter, and . . . combinations. Their location in the caves, and their subject matters and themes, suggest magico-religious sensitivities and rituals. The

paintings probably had something to do with rituals designed to increase the game supply and bring it under human control. They may also have had something to do with human fecundity and the curing of sickness. Religious rituals often center upon crises in human life, situations that provoke anxiety and threaten social stability. Where we find grave uncertainty about the food supply, or deep concern about sickness, or dread of death, or fears about the extinction of the group, there we are likely to find ritual.[15]

Sacraments

A sacrament is a corporate symbolic act. The word comes from the Latin *sacramentum*, which represented a soldier's token of loyalty. Sacraments represent the cultic continuity of the church from Jesus' time. *Baptism* is regarded as the universal mark of the Christian, transcending the particularities of denominational tradition. In some traditions—especially the Anglican, the Orthodox, and the Roman Catholic—*Holy Communion* is regarded as the heart of all Christian worship. It goes by various names—eucharist, the Lord's Supper, and the mass. In many congregations and traditions it is celebrated every Sunday or, in the Roman Catholic tradition, in every liturgy. Holy Communion is special to all Christian bodies except the Society of Friends, or Quakers.

In most traditions *baptism* happens early in a child's life in order to symbolize the prevenient grace of God, where God seeks this person long before she or he could in any way earn God's favor. It symbolizes, too, the public receiving of the baptized one into a community of Christians, who agree to nurture the child in faith. That receiving is not only into a particular congregation but into the whole family of God. Some traditions encourage an act of confirmation in which baptismal vows made in infancy are taken for one's own as an adult. In the tradition of the Baptists and of the Disciples of Christ, baptism is of believers and, therefore, participated in by youth or adults as they reach the declaration of faith stage.

The water symbolizes cleansing and forgiveness. The laying on of hands symbolizes the continuity and the promise of God's grace. Baptism is normally done in a Sunday service, when the whole congregation has gathered, so as to set the individual family in the broader social context and to symbolize the whole church's responsibility for the fate and future of the baptized.

The Consultation on Church Union suggested the following prayer for use in baptism. Much of the symbolism of the water is identified in this prayer.

We thank you, God, for water. By it you give life to plants and animals and all persons. By this gift you nourish us with life's necessities and you offer us cleansing and refreshment.

Through the waters of the Red Sea you led your people Israel out of slavery into the inheritance of a new land. To the waters of the River Jordan our Lord Jesus came to be baptized. Today we praise you because by water you enfold us in the death of Christ and from water you raise us, in a resurrection like his, into the power and peace of those who believe in him.

Calling upon your name, O God, we come to this water. By the power of your Holy Spirit, make it a cleansing flood that washes away sin and gives new life to these who today confess the name of Christ. Bind them into the Christian community of love, joy, and peace, destroying the hostilities that divide. As you did on Pentecost, baptize them in your Holy Spirit that they may be strong to do your work of reconciling love until that day when you make all things new.[16]

Baptism happens once. The sacrament of Holy Communion is an oft-repeated act. The various names given to this rite suggest its meaning. It is a eucharist, a giving thanks for God's love and presence in Jesus and for Jesus' atoning act. It is the Lord's Supper, the family gathering of those who, by blood and faith, belong to him. It is communion, the sharing and building of community. This community is not just the obvious local group who gather in a given place; for Worldwide Communion Sunday reminds us that it is the community of the church everywhere. And, as the notion of the communion of saints suggests, it is the continuity of the present gathered community with those who have shared the faith in other generations and places.

There are two points of origin for the service of communion. One is the last supper, when Jesus celebrated the Passover meal with his disciples on the first Maundy Thursday. The second source is the postresurrection appearance of Jesus to two disciples on the Emmaus road, as reported in Luke 24. Jesus became known to them in the breaking of bread after their common journey. The key text for the communion celebration is 1 Corinthians 11:23-32.

Word and sacrament have been intertwined throughout Christian history. Although sometimes one has been emphasized more than the other, they are interdependent. In the Protestant Reformation, Luther and Calvin emphasized the word as a recovery of biblical interpretation and understanding. For both these preachers, communion was part of their recommended order of worship for use in Wittenberg and in Geneva. In some ways the predominance of

Sacraments. . . . Use of a whole loaf of bread to be broken suggests the unity of the whole people. On Worldwide Communion Sunday try using breads from all over the world.

preaching over the Lord's Supper in American Protestantism re-
sulted from the scarcity of clergy on the frontier who could ad-
minister the sacraments.

In 1976 a United Methodist commission reported its findings with
a new order of worship that has its roots in John Wesley's own
practice. Interpreting why communion was recommended as part of
each Sunday worship service, the commission wrote:

> The celebration of the Thanksgiving Meal is a *way of doing*, not only a
> ritual order of words. Worship is far more than the right words in the
> right order, and much more than something "preached." Increasing
> numbers of Christians understand and desire worship to be a corporate
> action of the gathered community. The basic pattern presented here
> may enable us to experience more clearly this corporate enactment of
> the story and the mystery of the Christian faith. The action character of
> worship is especially evident in the sacraments of Baptism and the
> Lord's Supper. The sacraments are *eventful* and involve the body and
> all our senses, and not merely the hearing of words recited.[17]

Also, this commission recognized that communion would *not* be
part of the worship on every occasion and interpreted its mind
further:

> Whether or not the service on a given Sunday includes the Lord's
> Supper, it is important that we recover the basic shape and intent of the
> full order. The presence of Christ is known, by the aid of the Spirit, in
> the assembly gathered in his name, in Scripture and proclamation,
> prayer and praise. The full experience of the Word is completed in the
> celebration of the Meal. By this we recognize that Christ is present to
> his people in many ways.[18]

An order for communion is included in the Appendix of this book.
In it you will find these traditional elements: the thanksgiving,
words of institution, the actions of breaking the bread and drinking
the wine, acts of dedication and consecration. Because it is one of
the continuity forms in the church's liturgical life, people have come
to have a strong sense of expectation about the style and patterns of
the communion service. Even so, there are variations on the theme.
Maundy Thursday communion may differ from the communion
celebrated on Worldwide Communion Sunday.

One moving and empathetic way to do Worldwide Communion is
to divide the congregation proportionally, according to the popula-
tion of each continent. The Asia contingent will be large, while that
from North America comparatively small. Communion elements can

be distributed in amounts commensurate with the quantity of food consumed in each continent. In a dramatic way we are reminded of the accidents of birth and of the hunger pains in large sectors of the world community.

Not only are variations within the service itself possible and desirable, but the place in which one gives and receives the elements may also vary. For example, the congregation can gather around the table in the chancel, or persons can come to the altar and receive the elements kneeling, or the elements can be passed to persons while they are seated in the pews. Wherever the place, it is important that each one serve his or her neighbor rather than just take one's own elements. Be sure to arrange for someone to serve the celebrant. Offering the elements to one another conveys our caring for, our service to, and our communion with the other.

In many churches various members of the congregation take turns baking bread for communion. These persons bring the bread forward as part of the offering. In this way even the elements are expressive of the gift of the congregation. A single loaf is preferable to wafers or tiny squares of store-bought sliced bread, because it suggests the unity of the whole people—"out of the many grains, one loaf."

One liturgy of the eucharist catches some of this spirit:

> Blessed are you, Lord, God of all creation.
> Through your goodness we have this bread to offer,
> Which earth has given and human hands have made.
> It will become for us the bread of life.
>
> Blessed are you, Lord, God of all creation.
> Through your goodness we have this wine to offer,
> Fruit of the vine and work of human hands.
> It will become our spiritual drink.[19]

Baptism and Holy Communion have a number of things in common: both are rooted in Jesus' experience; each offers a faith invitation and seeks a response; both have physical elements, such as bread, wine, and water; each includes specific action, such as sprinkling of the water and the fraction of the bread; both are corporate acts; and each ends on a note of consecration and commissioning.

Creeds

The two most universal creeds are the Apostles' Creed and the Nicene Creed. In spite of its name, the Apostles' Creed cannot be traced to Jesus' earliest followers. The basic text of this creed goes by the nickname "Old Roman Symbol" (symbol is used here to mean a sign or expression of faith) and as such was probably used in the life of the early church during baptism. Note its use of the first person. Here is one translation:

> I believe in God, the Father almighty,
>> creator of heaven and earth.

> I believe in Jesus Christ, his only Son, our Lord.
>> He was conceived by the power of the Holy Spirit
>>> and born of the Virgin Mary.
>> He suffered under Pontius Pilate,
>>> was crucified, died, and was buried.
>> He descended to the dead.
>> On the third day he rose again.
>> He ascended into heaven,
>>> and is seated at the right hand of the Father.
>> He will come again to judge the living and the dead.

> I believe in the Holy Spirit,
>> the holy catholic Church,
>> the communion of saints,
>> the forgiveness of sins,
>> the resurrection of the body,
>> and the life everlasting.[20]

The Nicene Creed is an ancient creed also, probably predating the era of its name. At the Ecumenical Council of Nicea, in A.D. 325, a major argument about the nature of Jesus and his relationship to God took place. The key phrase, "One in being with the Father," reflects the outcome of that debate. Note the change from first-person singular to first-person plural:

> We believe in one God,
>> The Father, the Almighty,
>> maker of heaven and earth,
>> of all that is seen and unseen.

> We believe in one Lord, Jesus Christ,
>> the only Son of God,
>> eternally begotten of the Father,
>> God from God, Light from Light,
>> true God from true God,

begotten, not made, one in Being with the Father.
Through him all things were made.
For us and for our salvation
    he came down from heaven:
by the power of the Holy Spirit
    he was born of the Virgin Mary, and became man.
For our sake he was crucified under Pontius Pilate;
    he suffered, died, and was buried.
    On the third day he rose again
        in fulfillment of the Scriptures;
    he ascended into heaven
        and is seated at the right hand of the Father.
He will come again in glory to judge the living
        and the dead,
    and his kingdom will have no end.

We believe in the Holy Spirit, the Lord, the giver of life,
    who proceeds from the Father (and the Son).
    With the Father and the Son he is worshiped
        and glorified.
    He has spoken through the Prophets.
    We believe in one holy catholic and apostolic Church.
    We acknowledge one baptism for the forgiveness of sins.
    We look for the resurrection of the dead,
        and the life of the world to come. Amen.[21]

Although some elements of the two creeds differ, generally the differences reflect their circumstances of origin—the Apostles' being a statement of faith for baptism and the Nicene being a doctrinally oriented statement to settle a conflict. More importantly, the two faith statements share a number of similarities. They both contend that:
God is father, almighty, creator;
Jesus is son, Lord, born of Mary through the spirit, crucified, died, buried, risen, coming again, and judge.
Belief in the Holy Spirit
Belief in the church—holy and catholic (universal)
Belief in the forgiveness of sins
And belief in the resurrection.
John Calvin wrote that "creeds are to be sung, not said." By that he meant they are affairs of the believing heart, not tools for arguments. They are, as the Old Roman Symbol designation suggests, symbols of faith and of the faith community.
For many people, more contemporary statements are more ex-

pressive of their faith experience. For example, the United Church Statement of Faith (see page 16) and the statement of faith of the United Church of Canada reflect the modern idiom, while retaining much of the structure of the more classic creeds. Here is the United Church of Canada's statement:

> We are not alone; we live in God's world.
>
> We believe in God
>> who has created and is creating;
>> who has come in Jesus, to reconcile
>> and make new.
>
> We trust God
>> who calls us to be the church;
>> to love and serve others;
>> to seek justice and resist evil;
>> to proclaim Jesus, crucified and risen,
>> our judge and our hope.
>
> In life, in death, in life beyond death,
>> God is with us.
> We are not alone.
>
> Thanks be to God.[22]

Part of the beauty of the church's worship is in the interplay between the historic creeds and the new forms that emerge out of the congregation's common life.

In this chapter we have looked intensively at faith itself—its character and its embodiment in the life of a congregation. We have explored some of the forms that faith takes in both historical and contemporary terms. Faith and form are interdependent and in dialogue with each other. This is a continuing story. We shall explore it further as we look at environment, the Bible, music, movement, and education—other forms that faith takes. Each of us in her or his own way will continue the dialogue of faith and form, for that is the nature of the human experience.

Symbols of the Christian Year. . . . Planners of worship need to choose carefully and with fresh eyes the symbols they will use, for as symbols emerge out of the life of a people they become powerful expressions of faith.

CHAPTER 4

Symbols and Seasons of the Christian Year

We express ourselves as a people of faith in countless ways. Some of the rhythms of the spirit and some of faith's forms have been examined earlier. We turn now to take a closer look at our historic roots as conveyed in Christian symbols and in the church year. These forms have stood the test of time—a tribute to their authenticity and their contemporaneity.

Symbols

Planners of worship need to choose carefully and with fresh eyes the symbols they will use. Some symbols are a consistent part of the worship place, but even these need to be reexpressed and reentered. When Herbert Ginsburg and Silvia Opper interpret Jean Piaget's findings concerning human development, they are clear that "from two to four years the child begins to develop the ability to make something—a mental symbol, a word, or an object—stand for or represent something else which is not present."[1] As soon as we learn this representative element in human experience, we find that we live in a strong, symbolic world.

Some symbols, such as stop signs and rest room markers, are highly functional. Others, like smiley faces, are more aesthetic and touch the wellspring of the spirit and the psyche. Symbols like the cross often emerge naturally in the common experience of a community. A smile and a tear have universal meaning and require a minimum of explanation. Like language forms, they express agreement about meaning on the part of a community of people.

The fish symbol used by the early church is a good illustration of this. This symbol with the Greek word *Ixthus* became a secret greeting between Christians in a time when the state considered it treason to be a Christian. To someone outside the believing community, the drawing of the fish appeared to be simple doodling; however, to the believer, it expressed Christian conviction and identified a sister or a brother in the faith. *Ixthús* is the word for fish in Greek, the language of the New Testament. It symbolized for the believers these articles of faith:

I	Jesus	(Iēsoús)
X	Christ	(Christós)
TH	God's	(Theós)
U	Son	(Úiós)
S	Savior	(Sotéros)

The use of this symbol was a reminder of Jesus' call to discipleship, found in Mark 1:17.

Many symbols may be found in your sanctuary or elsewhere in your church building. Wherever they are they should be used to focus worship and as teaching resources. The worship leader should take both old and new symbols seriously. Old symbols have historic significance, with relatively fixed meanings for a congregation. We may build on these meanings or offer complementary images, such as other forms of the symbol from a different culture or a meaning that people haven't noticed before. But we should never treat such symbols flippantly. When creating new symbols we suggest that they come out of the common life and convey religious truth. Jesus did that superbly with a mustard seed, a coin, and a cross.

All symbols can be created in various art forms, including banners, and then be used for a long period of time or for a season. For instance, Suzanne Benton has developed the mask form as a vital way to dramatize a particular character.

We should be prepared for the fact that when presenting new symbols we may or may not be successful, because symbols perform different functions for people and our choices may conflict with others. Sometimes a new symbol works fine for a certain occasion but offers no permanent validation; in other circumstances a casual symbol may come to be widely accepted. Many times the new symbol takes hold because it is convincing, relevant, and the timing is right.

We should be quick to recognize symbols as they emerge in our common lives: Watergate and Proposition 13 are two illustrations. They are concrete events that convey a wider truth or meaning. However, we should use such emergent symbols carefully and should be aware of how easily they may become trite. Also, because they are powerful and emotionally loaded, they may blow up in our faces if people feel we are trivializing them or if we apply them in ways people consider illegitimate.

Symbols emerge out of the life of a people, and once they take form, they have their own lives; yet a continuing process of reentry into the symbolic world and a re-presentation of the symbol becomes necessary as time makes the symbol more remote from people's primary faith experience. Alfred North Whitehead observed that "knowledge, like fish, does not stay fresh." Neither does a symbol.

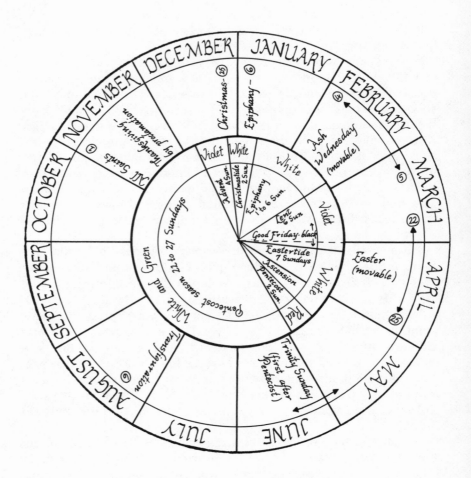

The Christian Year.[2] . . . The dimensions of human experience found in the Christian year will help us in planning worship and activities in the congregation's life.

The Christian Year

The Christian year is Jesus' journey. The year begins with *Advent*, which is the expectation of Jesus' birth, and a pilgrimage, concluding with *Christmas*. Then the year celebrates *Christmastide* for twelve days, ending in *Epiphany*. Several Sundays after Epiphany, the year moves into *Lent*, the drama of *Holy Week*, and the climax of *Easter*. Over the next fifty days we move to the birthday of the Christian church, which is *Pentecost*. Sundays in the remaining half year are referred to as *Trinity*, and represent days of faith and witness. This brings the year full cycle, to the beginning of Advent. Each day or season has its appropriate scriptural rootage and liturgical elements. Each has its relevance as a celebration in the theatre of the spirit.

The Christian year is tied in with the moods of the spirit and the dimensions of human experience. It begins with the expectation of birth and carries into the earliest stages of life. The Christmas story, for all its wonder and pageantry, is a reminder of the precarious actual character of human existence. The season of Lent reflects Jesus' days in the wilderness and is marked with the remembrance of his temptations. The ups and downs of the human spirit are reflected in the Christian year. Moreover, it is a dynamic, dramatic pilgrimage consonant with our own history. Stuart Hampshire's comments set the context for this:

> The essence of work, or of mere work is, and always has been repetition. But over most of known history the repetitions have been given significance by recurring celebrations of seasons and of work done, in feasts, ceremonies, enactments of myth and history, dramatic and musical performances, public manifestations of all kinds. If the repetitions of work are not given any kind of seasonal rhythm or pattern, because the beliefs, principally religious, associated with such rhythms have largely disappeared, then they remain mere repetitions, leaving a blank, an empty aging, an undifferentiated stretch of days and months, as in a prison before death.[3]

Advent and Christmas

The church year begins on the Sunday nearest November 30 with Advent, a word that means "to come." It is a time to prepare for the coming of the Christchild. Violet is the symbolic color for this period, denoting penitence, humility, and sometimes royalty. Advent celebrates the mystery of physical intimacy, conception, gestation, and incarnation—the touch of the divine in the midst of the human. The season expresses powerfully the moods of awe and wonder.

An advent wreath in both home and sanctuary is appropriate for the season. Usually the wreath has five candles; four are purple and one is white. It is circular, symbolizing the infinity of God, and it is green—the color of living things—which expresses the spirit of Christian hope. One of the purple candles is lighted four Sundays before Christmas. On each of the three successive Sundays an additional purple candle is lighted (the previously lit candles are often relighted before the service of worship begins). The four candles stand for hope, peace, love, and joy. Appropriate scriptures for the four Sundays are, respectively, Micah 5:2, Isaiah 9:6f., John 1:1-14, and Luke 1:46-55. The white candle is lighted on Christmas Eve. This candle represents Jesus as the light of the world, as expressed in John 1:1-9. The Christmas story, Luke 2:1-20, is appropriate for Christmas Eve. The Appendix offers an advent service for use in our homes.

The advent season is a beautiful and wonderful one for intergenerational participation. Workshops or work groups can prepare items for congregational worship and for family worship, such as advent calendars, wreaths, banners, decorations for the tree, a crèche, the star, and various characters of both Advent and Christmas stories. How about a birthday cake for Jesus—at home, in church, or in church school? Cookies and caroling can provide a special and wonderful example of caring—which is what Christmas is all about. Of course, nativity pageants and the performing of great musical works are essential parts of the season.

Halford Luccock describes an interesting tradition that developed eight centuries ago:

> One of the quaint bits of lore connected with the Christmas celebration is part of the history of the churches of twelfth-century Paris. There, on Christmas Sunday, the "people of low degree" filled the churches, rubbing shoulders with their "betters," the feudal aristocracy. When in the course of the service the Magnificat was read and the stirring words were pronounced . . . "[God] hath put down the mighty from their seats and exalted them of low degree," the folk "of low degree," recognizing their cue, would yell their heads off in approval, with a noise that almost lifted the roof. For long years this chaos reigned unconfined. Then in 1198 the bishop of Paris decreed that after seven yells— that medieval form of Amen—the clamor must stop. So thereafter the plain people had to content themselves with giving to the program of "exalting them of low degree" only seven rounds of applause.[4]

Think of an appropriate adaptation of the seven yells custom for your church!

One church celebrated an advent service that focused on disarmament. Beating swords into ploughshares and anticipating a Prince of Peace are appropriate themes for addressing this issue, and the church had to decide how to convey these essential themes of the Christmas scriptures in liturgical form.

Suitable banners were chosen, carried forward in the processional, and placed in the chancel. People costumed as puppets dramatically represented the conflicting images of violence and nonviolence; warmakers and skeletal death forms symbolized one alternative, while peace pilgrims suggested the other. The service included a conflict between the two powers, during which various people from the congregation led a litany that symbolized their own hopes amidst the turmoil.

Aluminum foil was used to construct a large missile, which overshadowed the cross in the chancel. At a key point in the service, children were asked to come into the chancel. They were identified as the future toward which choices must be made now. Later the children beat against the missile with broomsticks. (Is this how swords were beaten into ploughshares?) Almost miraculously, the now-defunct missile spilled out its innards—signs and symbols representing day care, health care, housing, recreational facilities, schools, and artistic ventures. These latter symbols expressed the very elements of human community that were denied by an over-commitment to missiles and militarism. Songs, hymns, scripture, prayers, and meditation conveyed the sense of choice between the two ways and emphasized the Christmas motifs of love and non-violent action.

Christmastide and Epiphany

Christmastide extends from December 24 to January 6, the twelfth night after Christmas, and includes Epiphany. This is a joyful period that catches the afterglow of Christmas. White is this season's color because it symbolizes joy and light. The theme of light can be especially meaningful at Christmastide. Use such passages as Isaiah 60:1, John 8:12, and Ephesians 5:8-10. This is an important time to share gifts with others. Many churches make special contributions to particular agencies that serve human need. How about a "light and bushel" ceremony, in which the motifs of Matthew 5:15 find liturgical expression? After the rush of the pre-Christmas period the worship moments of Christmastide can have special, enduring meaning.

During this season the old year ends and the new year begins. Some churches have a Watch Night, or New Year's Eve, service, where silence and the special environment of the sanctuary at night are featured. The liturgical elements by which we take responsibility for but also take leave of the events of the past year should be provided. It is an ideal time to use movement and pageantry to symbolize these events. For good or ill, all should be given into God's hands for safekeeping. A prayer vigil is an appropriate part of this night's service.

The Watch Night service provides an opportunity for New Year's resolutions to be made. These can be expressed orally as individuals come forward, or each worshiper can write his or her resolutions on a piece of paper and then carry it to the altar in an act of dedication. Persons could also write themselves a resolutions letter, which the church would return to them the following advent season. Further, some Watch Night services provide the means for people to rid themselves of events they want to let go. This can be done by writing the event on a piece of paper, sealing it, and then burning it in an appropriate container. Often such a service follows a New Year's Eve party. This mixture of hilarity and seriousness, balanced with letting go and quiet dedication, represents moods of our lives and of the gospel.

Churches of the Orthodox tradition celebrate Christmas on January 6. If there is an Orthodox church nearby, it can perhaps share some of the key elements of that ancient liturgy.

The essential Bible passage for Epiphany Sunday is Matthew 2, the saga of the Magi. Its motifs are the sharing of gifts, the universality of the Christian faith, and the ability of Jesus to transcend our differences of culture and distance. Matthew 2:13-23 describes the flight of the holy family into Egypt as a consequence of the threat of such an appealing faith to an insecure ruler. The whole passage offers dramatic opportunity for worship expression. For instance, three persons (women and men) can express in sermons what their contemporary gifts to Jesus would be.

The Epiphany season continues until Ash Wednesday. It celebrates the universality of Jesus and the implications of his message of love, peace, good will, and unity for the whole world. The key scripture is the experience of Simeon and Anna recorded in Luke 2:22-40. Epiphany is when the church's missionary task is emphasized. It is an ideal time to develop a special missionary project. It needs to have local dimensions, so that all who desire to do so can feel they have a stake in it. After all, the word Epiphany means "to manifest" or "to show forth." The Acts of the Apostles reflects the experiences of the earliest church as it left the bounds of its own cultural setting, so perhaps a project that would enable your congregation to do the same should be chosen.

Lent and Easter

Lent begins with Ash Wednesday, which is the fortieth day before Easter—not counting Sundays—or actually, the fortieth day before Holy Week. The forty days symbolize Jesus' temptation and fasting as recorded in Matthew 4:1-10 and in Luke 4:1-13. The color for Lent is purple, suggesting penitence, humility, and empathy.

The lenten season puts us in touch with life's journeys—with temptation, pilgrimage, faith and faithfulness, discipline, and the flowering of human experience. We sense the fragile triumph of Palm Sunday, knowing how good our victories taste, yet how full of foreboding they may be. Holy Week is about loyalty, choices, trust, pain, promise, and hope. It is also about human courage and resilience and the power of God to turn the bleakest moments into ones of promise. Those who believe recognize the risen Christ as they journey together on the road. We know that need and feeling in our own journeying.

Ash Wednesday gets its name from the tradition of burning palms from the preceding year's Palm Sunday on that day. The ashes of these palms are used to make the sign of the cross on the foreheads of believers. One adaptation of this practice that is widely used in Catholic churches is to ask people to express either their lenten commitments or their fears on paper. These papers are burned in a fireplace or a brazier, and the ashes are used in the same manner as the palm ashes.

The day before Ash Wednesday is called Shrove Tuesday. It is a day closely associated with Mardi Gras and is one of hilarity and festivity before the solemnity and self-denial of Lent. Somehow we wish the celebrations of the lenten season could be made to express both the mirth and the tragedy that were so fully part of Jesus' experiences. The classic Greek masks of comedy and of tragedy catch this dynamism.

If you are preparing a series of services for Lent, treat them as a pilgrimage. Use characters who make their way with Jesus—such as Peter, Mary Magdalene, James and John, and Luke—or modern pilgrims like Martin Luther King Jr., Dag Hammarskjöld, Mother

Teresa, Thomas Merton, and Dorothy Day. One church used characters from *The Wiz* to focus the theme; each of the lenten Sundays one character appeared in full costume: innocent, trusting Dorothy in search of a home; the lion in search of courage; the tin man seeking a heart; and the scarecrow seeking a brain. Each character's presence gave focus and excitement to persistent lenten themes. The season obviously lends itself to dance and drama, as we explore the meaning of Jesus' temptations and the elements of the Christian life. Using early Christian symbols and narrative stained glass can also enhance our storytelling and celebration.

Explore in sermon and service the seven deadly sins, along with the seven cardinal virtues, using such themes as:

> Pride and Wisdom
> Envy and Justice
> Anger and Temperance
> Sloth and Courage
> Avarice and Faith
> Gluttony and Hope
> Lust and Love[5]

Because Lent emphasizes self-denial as in, "What are you giving up for Lent?" special offerings like One Great Hour of Sharing are an essential part of our celebrations. Perhaps there are things we can commit ourselves *to do* that reflect the discipline of caring and doing. For example, we can write letters to or visit shut-ins. Also, it is a crucial time to do a project or to plan in such a way that the pilgrimage toward Easter will be dramatic and real. We may want to undertake a historical project or a local service effort; or it may be an occasion for special educational efforts. It can be an important time to create something, such as banners or a pageant or musical work, that will be part of the Holy Week or Easter services.

The great scriptures of Holy Week speak for themselves. Palm Sunday, the day reminiscent of Jesus' triumphal entry into Jerusalem, is recorded in all four Gospels, with varied emphases upon the borrowed donkey, the pageantry of the procession, the worshiping crowds, and the waving palms. It's the old "riding for a fall" motif.

Maundy Thursday puts us in touch with some of the deepest human emotions. We see a conflict of authority as the movement growing out of Jesus' mission challenges the religious establishment and the political powers of the time. Curiously, it is these powers who saw themselves under siege, not Jesus' little band of disciples.

We experience the challenge to loyalty and the threat of betrayal. Jesus' followers had responded to his call in fair-weather times, but now the times were foul. Blame was easy. Loyalty was hard. Doubt and despair waited in the wings. Would his followers respond to his call now? Where was faith in all this? Where was belief in a tomorrow?

These hard events have a sense of inevitability about them. Jesus' Maundy Thursday prayer rings true to our own experiences with the dark side of our lives: "If it be possible, let this cup pass from me; nevertheless, not as I will, but as thou wilt [Matt. 26:39]." Yet Maundy Thursday praying includes the remarkable verses in John 17, where Jesus' praying was primarily for the well-being of his companions on the journey. Footwashing sealed his concern and caring.

Maundy Thursday reminds us afresh of our vital Jewish roots. The first supper was a Passover celebration, expressive of God's intervention to protect the children of Israel in Egypt from annihilation (see Exodus 12:1-20).

Maundy Thursday places us face to face with the fact and inevitability of death. Celebrating the Last Supper gives us a sense of the solidarity of those who care even though it is marked by the shadow of betrayal; death is finally a solitary act, generally without nobility. Jesus' agony in the garden reminds us that death is hard and unwelcome. From the perspective of Maundy Thursday it appears purposeless and stupid.

The word Maundy comes from the Latin *mandatum,* "to command," and recalls Jesus' last night gift: "This is my commandment, that you love one another as I have loved you [John 15:12]." As you plan for Maundy Thursday try to catch up this commandment and its various moods and meanings in symbolic forms and acts. It is, of course, a time for communion. Footwashing is very appropriate. Praying for one another is dynamic. Motifs of light and darkness will be strong; even in darkness one candle should remain lighted to symbolize the hope of Easter. To emphasize that Maundy Thursday is a time for quiet, individual meditation, people traditionally leave the sanctuary at their own pace, so that each can give the service and its somber mood her or his own closure. There is no postlude and no pomp. Often an all-night prayer vigil leading into Good Friday will take place, with each person on the list, in turn, praying for a half hour or an hour.

Good Friday is a strange day, represented by black. It seems odd to call the day "good" when the worst things that can happen in life transpired that day. No one will take responsibility for the events. An unruly mob, wanting blood, is turned loose. The powers of religion and state conspire to destroy a perceived threat. Jesus' friends run away. He is murdered in a horribly cruel way. Darkness reigns.

Faith is the only thing that can find any good in the day; for beyond its ugliness there is the hope of Easter, beyond its betrayal is the promise of new community and fierce loyalty, and beyond the extinguishing of a threat to principalities and powers is a force that turns the world upside down.

Traditionally, the seven last words of Jesus have been used in Good Friday services. These phrases are:

> Father, forgive them; for they know not what they do (Luke 23:34).

> Today you will be with me in Paradise (Luke 23:43).

> Woman, behold your son! Son! Behold your mother! (John 19:26f.).

> My God, my God, why hast thou forsaken me? (Mark 15:34).

> I thirst (John 19:28).

> It is finished (John 19:30).

> Father, into thy hands I commit my spirit (Luke 23:46).

These are not simply the collected words of a man in the slow throes of death; they are reflective of eternal truths and basic human necessities that penetrate to the heart of the faith experience.

With its stations of the cross every Roman Catholic sanctuary is a Good Friday gallery. The fourteen stations are like stops on a train's journey and duplicate the Via Dolorosa, or "the way of suffering," which Jesus traveled. These portrayals bid us take the journey in our imagination as someday we will in actuality.

A large wooden cross may be used to dramatize the Good Friday story and to enable people to participate in its meaning. Each worshiper is given a nail and a card. On the card each person writes a sin or an act that comes to mind. At an appropriate moment each person nails his or her card to the cross in order to show that even today we participate in the sinning for which Jesus died. Thus Good Friday becomes a contemporary event.

Easter is powerful partly because of the drama of the events that precede it, and partly because the season coincides with the coming of spring, the rebirth of life. The word Lent is taken from an old English word for "spring," and the date of Easter is determined by the spring equinox. Even Easter eggs reflect the promise of new life. The season's color is white, denoting purity.

The Easter event is full of delightful surprises. The tomb is empty. It is to women that this news is revealed. Jesus appears to them first and then later to the scattered men of his retinue. He meets them at breakfast, on the road, and as they break bread together, the dreadful occurrences of the past week are set aside in acts of faith. The biblical word is true!

Easter is an evangelism event par excellence. It is a stirring call to faith. The struggle for rebirth is triumphant. A second chance has been granted. Whether one asked for it or not, faith is there, claiming a response. "Will you stand up for Jesus?" The time is now. Let the trumpets play. Sing hymns of joy and triumph. In prayer, litany, and celebrative acts proclaim that death is set aside and new life is at hand. Christ has died for our sins; let us be energized in that. The cross is there but it is empty. Let our banners symbolize our own resurrection journey from the cocoon to the caterpillar to the butterfly.

Easter worship should give us as much chance as possible to celebrate the diverse meanings of the event. Flowers denote new life and spring. The color of clothing, vestments, banners, and processional can convey the multisplendored sense of the new life bursting out all over. A special offering links us with human need and possibility. Traditional symbols—eggs, cross, lilies—add their special touch.

"Christ is risen!"

"He is risen indeed!"

"Alleluia!"

The Congregational Church of Fullerton, California found a way not only to say the words but to send them. A word like "Rejoice" or "Joy" or "Shalom" was spelled out in two-feet-high tissue paper letters and was attached to a balsa batten. Balloons were filled with helium and then tied to the batten. During the service, members of the congregation wrote their own Easter messages on tissue paper. After the service in the sanctuary was concluded, the congregation recessed to the parking lot, where the words were released into the air to make their own way and bring Easter into the lives of those who would be where the batten would eventually land. This is a colorful and uplifting way to set one's Easter hopes aloft with cheers and good wishes.

Pentecost and Trinity

The seven Sundays between Easter and Pentecost are called the first or the second or whatever Sunday after Easter. The intervening fifty days mark a special celebration of the resurrection events and the post-Easter events of the disciples. During this period the disciples moved from being students to becoming evangelists who shared the gift of new life in Jesus.

Pentecost is a Greek term for the Jewish Feast of Weeks, which occurs fifty days after the offering of the barley sheaf during the observance of Passover. This Jewish festival denotes new beginnings and the sense of God's presence in nature and history. The convergence of these two festivals gives us another marvellous opportunity to express our common roots in Judaism.

Pentecost, described in Acts 2, celebrates the gift of the Holy Spirit to bless and empower the infant church. This gift is the spiritual energy that Jesus gave to Christians to keep their life going. When we celebrate Pentecost we receive and renew that gift. The New Testament offers several meanings for Holy Spirit, such as comforter, revealer, advocate, and breath. Out of the gift of the Holy Spirit in our church's life come the gifts that the people have—tongues, music, prophecy, talents, dreams, passion, and the possibility of community. The liturgical color for Pentecost is red, conveying the fire, the passion of the Spirit giving birth.

One church that had anticipated Pentecost a long time beforehand asked each member to figure out what gift he or she wanted to make available for a big auction party. Some people made things and others promised to do things. Each found a way to express a gift to the church. The money that was raised was used to balance the church's budget and for a mission project. The Spirit was alive and well in this church—and the budget was healthier!

Pentecost is also a birthday party. We celebrate the birthday of the Christian church. The liturgical possibilities are endless. Somehow the day seems unnecessarily solemn in many churches. It needs to focus on the new, the surprising, the serendipitous in our lives. The Holy Spirit meets us—and we begin again. The day of Pentecost is a "we-day." It is about us. The people of God are gathered here and there to worship and to serve. It's our birthday and everybody counts. Balloons, streamers, and banners are called for.

The day is also one on which many churches confirm members. It's a good faith-day. Confirmation celebrates the continuity of God's grace and the promise of new life—fitting themes for a day we use to proclaim the gift of the Spirit and the birthday of the church.

The Sundays following Pentecost, until Advent, are known as the first or the second or whatever Sunday after Pentecost, or the first or the second Sunday in Trinity. The color is green, denoting continuing life.

The season, in part, replays the expanding life of the Christian church after its Pentecost empowerment. It also recalls the sense of God's continuing presence as creator, redeemer, and sustainer of people and the world. It is an expression of the unity and the forms in which the human community experiences God as parent, incarnate presence, and empowering spirit.

This liturgical season is a time of planning and of continuing work. Many churches have their annual meetings during this period. The interplay of the ongoing life of the Spirit with summer, the Fourth of July, Labor Day, and the beginnings of autumn represents the dynamic of a living faith. Although the Sundays are called the "blank" Sunday after Pentecost, in a sense, they should be called the "blank" Sunday in Pentecost, for they are Sundays in the life of the Spirit—after birth!

In this chapter our contention has been that the Christian church's life should be rooted in the church's history. Our current events should reflect that history as conveyed through the Christian year, so that we become grounded in what we do. We recommend that these motifs be used in planning worship and activities in the congregation's life. That dynamic life is reflected in the words of Ecclesiastes 3:1-8:

> For everything there is a season, and a time for
> every matter under heaven:
>> a time to be born, and a time to die;
>> a time to plant, and a time to pluck up
>>   what is planted;
>> a time to kill, and a time to heal;
>> a time to break down, and a time to build up;
>> a time to weep, and a time to laugh;
>> a time to mourn, and a time to dance;
>> a time to cast away stones, and a time to
>>   gather stones together;
>> a time to embrace, and a time to refrain from
>>   embracing;
>> a time to seek, and a time to lose;

a time to keep, and a time to cast away;
a time to rend, and a time to sew;
a time to keep silence, and a time to speak;
a time to love, and a time to hate;
a time for war, and a time for peace.

Environment for Worship. . . . The space in which worship happens comes to be special for us—not so much for itself but for the meanings we come to associate with it.

CHAPTER 5

Environment for Worship

Webster identifies three key meanings of the word environment. The first is surroundings; literally, the environs in which something happens. This has to do with the physical place of worship.

A second meaning is "the surrounding conditions, influences, or forces that influence or modify."[1] This has to do with the use of the senses and the atmosphere of worship.

A third meaning is "the aggregate of social and cultural conditions that influence the life of an individual or community."[2] This has to do with the cultural and the historical dimensions of our worship.

The pattern of our common celebration shapes our life as a people and as individuals. The space in which worship happens comes to be special for us—not so much for itself but for the meanings we come to associate with it. Choose your worship space with these criteria in mind:

First, it must be aesthetically pleasing. As an art form, it must come off as authentic, true, and imaginative; not as bizarre, incomplete, shoddy, or inauthentic.

Second, it must draw us beyond ourselves, into realms of spirit, imagination, and caring. It should convey the awe of splendor, a sense of ultimate mystery, and it should help our spirits to soar.

Third, it must reflect a sense of community for, after all, according to scripture, "we are members one of another." Architecture and design can help convey that sense of belonging, but they must do it in a way that leaves room for the individual. Our self-transcendence cannot be an obliteration of self!

Fourth, through symbolic form, it must put us in touch with anchor points of the Christian heritage and experience. Ideally, they should be expressed in an open, inviting way, so that our entry into the meaning of symbolic form is expansive and challenging. We should be able to say, "Wow!"—not, "Oh, yeah, there's the cross again."

No space or environment can fully contain these elements in and of itself, but we can design space so that it helps us reach toward the meanings our faith seeks to communicate. The space should enable a sense of meeting: divine Word with our experience; symbolic form with life meaning; person with person; and each of us with God.

If our worship is long on preaching and short on ritual, we will fail to appreciate the importance of the aesthetic dimension of worship. The word aesthetic actually means to perceive the character of the beautiful. Its components are visual, emotional, tactile, sensual, intuitive, shapely, and relational.

Obviously, a key element of the aesthetic is beauty. Although worship space uses color and form to lift our spirits and to heighten our sense of the lovely and the good, beauty need not be saccharine, plastic, or excessive. Instead, it is a quality through which our spirits are lifted beyond the ordinary. Let us enhance our place of celebration with flowers, banners, symbols, color, movement, light, and sound. These are not add-ons to Bible, pulpit, or altar. Each element has its own integrity and place, so that it complements the others in ways that may raise the total aesthetic impression. Each needs to be savored on its own terms.

Every space has a skeletal structure and a particular shape that may be nondescript or intentionally symbolic. We cannot always control the structure and shape of given space, but we can make choices about how to use it. If the shape of the space we intend to use is right for our purposes, let us use it to augment our mode of worship. If not, let us reshape it. Paint, wallpaper, light, and color can help. Banners do wonderful things for bare walls; one of their pluses is that they get across intended meanings. Also, they can be changed as new symbols become important.

The aesthetic includes style. Style may be formal, informal, or flexible, but it always offers its own strengths and limitations. In some sanctuaries it would not occur to one to speak above a whisper, while in others the conversation of the living room is reproduced. Some worship environments are nondescript, while others are ornate and elaborate. Certainly, the architecture of the building determines most of what will happen in that space, but style includes other components as well. Style is also the way one does things: it is dialogical or communal or individual or authoritarian. It is affected by whether the focus is more on music than on preaching. It involves the patterns of congregational participation and whether change or consistency predominate in worship. These elements of style grow out of the life of the congregation, and they are greatly enhanced when the worship leader conveys a style of leading that is both comfortable and effective.

Architectural style and worship style are interrelated. They shouldn't scream at each other, for if they do the dissonance creates awkwardness and disharmony.

The environment for our worship creates the context in which spirit meets spirit and in which our hopes are transformed into new being. The Bible is clear about this in calling us to worship God in the beauty of holiness.

Architectural Elements

This is not a book on architecture, but some comments regarding the subject are essential. Architecture is a form of art and includes all the elements of any art form: media, shape, texture, color, light, boundaries, meaning statement, and the relationship between elements. Samuel H. Miller believes that "faith without art is dumb."[3] How, then, can architecture speak? What will it say?

Architecture, like any other art form, has its traditions and conventions; for example, certain things belong to the Gothic, the Romanesque, the New England Colonial, or the Spanish tradition. It is important to be clear about which architectural tradition one is dealing with and to know the givens. There may be adaptations, but they are actually variations on a theme.

Louis Sullivan's dictum that "form follows function" is a principle to keep in mind. It means that purpose and use must be settled before architectural form is chosen.

All architecture has a utilitarian role—to house people and functions, to gather related elements, to enhance particular activity, and to symbolize purpose. Specifically, the function of church space is to provide for church functions: worship, fellowship, meeting, business, education, outreach, food preparation, and sanitation. To complement the utilitarian role, church space creates the statement of the transcendent and the interface of the eternal and the human. Architect Edward A. Sovik contends that "art is a means not simply of accomplishing a technical intention, but of dealing with ideas, and at its most serious, with the disclosure of truth."[4]

In a stirring article Paul Goldberger, the architecture critic of *The New York Times*, wondered about the relationship between church

architecture and contemporary art in general. He wondered why
recent church buildings contributed so little to the shaping of contemporary architectural traditions. The reason, he mused, may be
that

> we have so rarely been willing to undertake the anguish, the difficulty,
> of thinking about what we want out of a religious building, and no
> kind of building project is more demanding of that kind of basic,
> serious thinking before any success comes.[5]

Goldberger went on to explore his theme further. He contended
that

> too many churches represent answers. I would prefer if more of them
> represented questions, if their architects had been more concerned
> with making forms and spaces that would encourage us to think, to
> look, and to wonder rather than forms and spaces that offer easy
> answers. I do not think that the offering of easy answers is what re-
> ligion is, or should be, about.[6]

The great challenge to the congregation that would build or
renovate space is to envision purpose and program. This involves
reaching toward agreement on faith and meaning statements and on
the function of space. It can be enhanced by visits to various church
buildings and a review of pictures of spatial treatments. While the
relationship is dialogical, an architect cannot and should not be
expected to provide those questions and answers of faith and program. Behind a good building is a vital, well-conceived program/
function statement and a good architect.

Some key elements should be part of the planning. We have already spoken of beauty, authenticity, and challenge to the human
spirit as environmental factors. Further, we should be aware that the
building itself will make a faith statement. The building needs to be
in tune with the geographical context in which it is placed and
should foster both vertical and horizontal relationships. Efficient
energy use and accessibility for people with handicaps are essential.

Our goal as church planners is twofold—we should know what we
want and see that we get it. This will happen in the mutuality of our
relationship with the architect. It is not an architect's job to write the
church's ticket. The church has a right to expect an architect to
develop and carry out an artistic concept that provides shelter, function space, and symbolic statement. In turn, an architect has a right

to expect a client to be clear about purpose, style, form, and function, as well as to judge drawing and plan for their adequacy. Here is the second key point of decision-making: Our definition of adequacy has to do with whether or not the treatment reflects our intentions about meaning statement, beauty, utility, access, cost, and style.

Parkway Presbyterian Church, in Corpus Christi, Texas, provides an excellent example of a comprehensive, long-range planning process. At the outset two committees were formed: one on arts and the other on architecture. They went back to the early church, in the days before Constantine, to learn what churches were like and what worship was like, because they became convinced that after Constantine the church moved into what they think of as an "edifice complex." The result of their planning is an aesthetically rich church in a building whose architecture reflects a concern for community and worship. The building is remarkably suited to its landscape and to the concern of members of the congregation.

In thinking of space to convey "the work of the people," it is important not just to think of the sanctuary. For example, First Presbyterian Church, in Stamford, Connecticut—sometimes called "the fish church" because of the striking shape of its sanctuary—provides three interesting links with tradition in an imaginative way. One is the history walk, which is a series of stepping-stones between the parking lot and the sanctuary entrance that give the name, location, and dates of important figures throughout Christian history. There is an inside wall that displays stones gathered from significant places in the biblical and Christian world, such as Bethlehem, Jerusalem, Ephesus, Rome, and Wittenberg. The third link with tradition is a stone wall in the church's front yard, which includes key dates in the history of the town and the state. With these treatments, one journeys the church's territory with a sense of being set in the midst of a vital and long historical venture.

More often than not, you will be modifying or adapting space that already exists. A major change in look or focus can come with a bucket of paint, plants, paintings, sculpture, and hangings. Lighting decisions can make a world of difference. Lights should be correlated with daytime and nighttime function, and there should be a difference between general, all-purpose lighting and focused lighting. Spotlights on key areas and focal points can accent faith symbols. The use of color provides for flexibility. The choir, the congregation, the worship leader, and the altar all need careful lighting treatment. Lights on a rheostat increase choices. Controls for all lighting should be located both in the chancel and at the rear of the sanctuary. Ease of access to these controls is essential.

In planning for sound treatment, consider the elements of worship that are dependent upon good sound. Remember that different levels of sound are necessary in a full and in an empty house, and that a system should provide for acoustical and aural flexibility.

In making lighting and sound decisions, see what others are doing, get their evaluation, and shop around. Get people to help who are lighting professionals, and sound designers and technicians. Don't depend on people for whom light and sound are simply a hobby. Too many congregations build a beautiful structure and then compromise on sound and lighting. The medium is the message. Don't compromise on light or sound.

As you build or remodel, plan with the present in mind, but also consider the future. What flexibility is there for placement of worship leaders? Where will the choir be? Is there space to process and recess? Are choir and organist in view of each other? Is the choir divided? Are robing facilities nearby? If there is (or is to be) a pipe organ, is there easy access to the pipes?

Is the seating stationary? Are pews in direct sunlight or drafts? If there is a garden seeable from the sanctuary, does it have suitable sunlight and drainage?

Are there enough electrical outlets and circuits in the proper locations for theatrical, dance, and audiovisual use? Can light bulbs be replaced easily? Is there storage area available for equipment, robes, and communionware?

Is the narthex arranged so that all its noise does not travel into the sanctuary? Are rest rooms accessible to worship leaders and to the congregation? Are there provisions for handicapped persons?

Are there present or potential facilities available for dance? for theatre? A resilient wood floor that will not give dancers shin splints is a must. How can we expect people to leap in Christian joy when they're going to come down on a thin layer of carpet over solid concrete?

Space and form should be developed in a way that makes it inclusive. A person who is confined to a wheelchair should have easy access. Someone who is hard of hearing should have amplification available. Provisions should be made for the visually and the physically handicapped. A Bible, hymnbook, or church bulletin printed in Braille should be considered for the blind who worship with you. If there are deaf persons in the congregation, arrangements should be made to have the spoken part of the worship service signed.[7]

Don't forget that church people come in all ages and sizes. A young child will feel like this is his or her space if the forms, heights, and perspectives of the young are really evident.

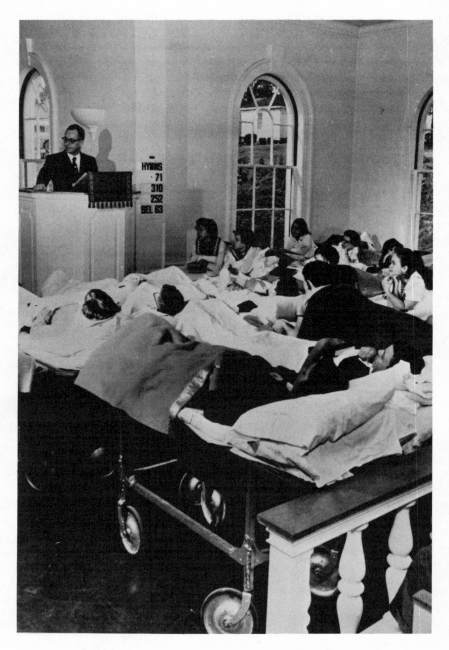

Architectural Elements. . . . Space and form should be developed so that it can be inclusive of handicapped persons.

The environment should reflect many ethnic and racial perspectives, even though in most churches one tradition will predominate. It is important to convey the feeling that we are part of a six-continent family, made one in Christ through the use of art, language, and symbols from various racial and cultural backgrounds.

Attention must be given as well to the problem of sexism. Because the majority of biblical and historical leaders have been males, it is very easy to create oral, symbolic, and artistic statements that exclude women. Androgynous, male, and female forms and symbols should be used.

A variety of resources are available to help a congregation delve more deeply into program definition prior to work with an architect. Edward A. Sovik's book, *Architecture for Worship*, provides a thoughtful overview of the subject.[8] *Focus: Building for Christian Education*, by Mildred C. Widber and Scott Turner Ritenour, reviews the various elements of that aspect of church program.[9] The fall 1978 issue of the *Journal of Current Social Issues* reviews the Fourth International Congress of Art, Architecture, Religion, and the Environment. Two Presbyterian church bodies have produced a series of multimedia kits on worship and the arts; the one on architecture is especially valuable for a congregation facing building or remodeling decisions.[10] *The Energy-efficient Church* provides guidelines on meeting the energy crisis.[11]

Shaping the Worship Atmosphere

Walk into the worship space as though you had never been there before. Look at it from a variety of positions and angles. Relax and settle into the space. Then ask yourself: What images and moods does it convey? What does it smell like? What does it look like? Is there a visual focus? Do you feel alone? Where are the sources of light? Does it make you feel comfortable? Is it inspiring? Does it draw your body and being into a new realm of imaginative reverence? Is it cluttered? Is it bare?

If the answers to these questions are to your liking, encourage others to enter as you have entered, and let the space lift the spirit and sustain the aura of worship. If, on the other hand, the space offers no aesthetic grace of its own, give attention to ways to transform it. Entering into the worship space can happen in a variety of ways. One way is to create certain passageways as trails of silence and anticipation to the worship meeting space. Another is for the whole worshiping body to form a processional, accompanied by

Shaping the Worship Atmosphere. . . . We can design space so that it helps us reach toward the meanings our faith seeks to convey. Clockwise: Chapel Hill United Church of Christ, Camp Hill, PA; circular altar; First Congregational Church, Cedar Falls, IA; St. Sophia Orthodox Cathedral, Los Angeles, CA.

banners, led by the choir, and singing a familiar hymn. More often people will come into the worship space singly or in groups over a period of time. The first people who enter the space are the ushers. Be intentional about how they enter and, in turn, help others to enter. Ushers can assist the desired mood if their spirit and style carries your intention to the worshipers whom they greet and seat. Bulletins can provide reading material to focus on symbols, theme, or mood. For instance, if there is a symbol of the day, begin calling attention to it with a picture in the narthex and related material in the bulletin.

The narthex, in fact, is a very important environmental center. It is the first location in which people have a sense of being inside holy space. Often, however, it is a place of clutter and confusion; it does not appear to be a preparatory setting for worship. One can change this by both appearance and the stance of ushers and greeters. Posters can convey church events, symbols, and history. Nametags for ushers and greeters impart a note of acquaintanceship that particularly enables newcomers to feel more at home. A cordial but serious stance on the part of greeters helps the entering worshipers to make the transition from the outside world to the theatre of the spirit.

Hopefully, the worship environment should touch all five senses. Our planning should address these *sight* questions: What do we want people to see? What meanings will visual form convey? The first letter of John talks of sight and the other senses: "That which was from the beginning, which we have heard, which we have seen with our eyes, which we have looked upon and touched with our hands, concerning the word of life—the life was made manifest, and we saw it [1:1-2]."

Obviously, we see the space in which worship happens. This space holds things for us to observe—color, shape, size, order, dust, faces, and symbols. There are some pragmatic questions to be addressed: Can people really see? Is there adequate light to read the bulletin? Is the sun glaring in people's eyes? Is attention paid to mood and general lighting? How are candles used? Has someone been assigned to operate the lights? Such a person should not be conspicuous. The lighting mood should be set before the first worshiper arrives.

The visual sense of worship can be enhanced by adding special dimensions on occasion, such as balloons, candles, symbols, masks, ashes, and flowers. Use of color is of utmost importance. In fact, the church's whole history can be told in the color of stoles and altar cloths. Purple is the color of Advent. White is used for Christmas

Day and for Epiphany. Purple is also used for the lenten season. White is the color for Easter and for the six Sundays in Eastertide. Black is appropriate on Maundy Thursday and on Good Friday. Red symbolizes the brilliance of Pentecost. Green is the color for the Sundays following Trinity Sunday, from the second Sunday after Pentecost until the beginning of Advent. One commercial set of stoles offers the following patterns: lamb and cross on purple; the word PAX and the cross on white; dove and circle on red; triangle and three crowns on green. Such color and symbol patterns heighten our visual celebration and identification.

Whether it is loud or is the "sound of silence," the sense of *sound* is strongly present. Some sounds are quite intentional—music, speaking, movement. Others are extraneous—the neighbor's lawn mower, moving cars, children at play—or spontaneous—applause, a gasp, a testimonial, a dropped offering plate. We cannot anticipate them all, but we should allow for them in our planning. If silent prayer is difficult because of neighbor sounds, do a bidding prayer and include the sounds as part of the praying. In planning for the sense of sound consider such practical matters as hearing aids, use of a good sound system, speaking loudly and clearly, and giving particular notice to diction when singing.

Worship planning should give careful attention to the elements of *touch* that we want to happen—a handshake or an embrace; a greeting; the feel of our hands against the props of worship—and to whether or not the seating is comfortable. Here we deal with the texture of the worship atmosphere. Footwashing is practiced by some churches as a separate ritual, or as part of communion, or within the Maundy Thursday rite (see John 13:1-17). Washing of hands may be substituted for footwashing. Sometimes when this is done, hand lotion is used as part of the pattern of cleansing.

The practical issues of touch are whether people are too hot or too cold, and whether seating is comfortable. We also hope that people will feel touched personally by the moods and the meaning of the worship experience. To touch the heart is to embrace the spirit.

The sense of *smell* is often neglected. Some smells are predictable, like mustiness, flowers, perspiration, and fresh air. Others are optional, like candles burning and food. If the sense of smell cannot be reached in any significant way, encourage people to imagine the smells of the holy.

The sense of *taste* comes into play especially during communion. Some churches include an agape meal once a month as part of the worship service. People bring fruit, bread, cheese, and wine, and share around the table as part of the liturgy.

There is a sixth sense—*intuition*. We cannot program it, but it is there. Deep within us there is response to space: Is it friendly or alien? Is it benign or exciting? Does it lead us beyond ourselves? Is it trivial? Is it banal? Our intuition will answer for us. We should "trust our gut" and shape space so that it helps our sixth sense to soar.

Elizabeth Cogburn comments on the elements she uses in preparing for a celebration:

> Being a very earthy person myself, I always invite the elements. I go out and find things in preparation for the ceremony that represent the earth, air, fire, and water. I give great attention to gathering these things, deciding what they should be, knowing myself to be made of these same elements.[12]

The five senses and intuition should be kept in mind as we choose the elements of the worship environment. There are a variety of ways to do this. It is a good idea to develop dependable components of the worship environment—some symbols that stand for something old and others which represent something new. Light, life, and color should always be conveyed by the environment. The Bible will be there. Banners will change. Somehow we must symbolize both continuity and the presence of a God who makes all things new.

Don't Forget the Church Bulletin

The worship folder containing the order of worship is an essential ingredient in the environment and contributes to the aesthetics of worship. It not only tells us what to do when but provides some of the rationale for worship elements. In addition to the worship order and any explanation that might enhance worship participation, it should offer introductory material to focus the day, the occasion, and the service. It may list alternate hymn texts. Also, the bulletin needs to be seen as a means by which key elements in the life of the faith community are shared—meeting notices, life passages of people, future worship plans, and important community concerns.

The bulletin has an aesthetic function: to set the tone and mood of the service. Introductory statements can provide meditation and background material for the day, the event, or the season. If we want people to enter the sanctuary in silence and to begin their part of the service with a reflective attitude, resources that will enhance this feeling should be given at the beginning of the bulletin. This lenten piece is an illustration:

Let me keep Lent.
Let me not kneel and pray,
Forego some trifle every day,
Fast—and take sacrament—
And then,
Lend tongue to slander, hold ancient grudge,
Deny
The very Lord whom I would glorify.

Let me keep Lent.
Let my heart grow in grace.
Let thy light shine till my illumined face
Will be a testament
Read by all . . .
That hate is buried; self-crucified; new-born
The spirit that shall rise on Easter morn.
Let me keep Lent.[13]

A quote from a play, a story, or a poem can be used. There are many poetry anthologies. Play scripts can be found in most libraries. Often the newspaper is a source of quotable material.

When it comes to basics, the folder should assume nothing. It should provide instructions dealing with what is happening and what is expected of the worshiper. Let it carry as much of the interpretive freight as possible, so that the worship can go forward "without commercials." The listing of music and the text of quotes should be double-checked for accuracy. Incorrect references make a bad impression.

The bulletin should be done with taste, so as to be inviting. The copy should be clear, not too long, and should express the style of the congregation, whether chatty or formal. It should present an attractive appearance through the use of artwork or through the quality of its layout. Churches and services have different moods and styles, and the worship form should be consistent with them. Have you ever noticed how menus differ from one restaurant to another? All have the same basic function: to answer the questions of what and how much. Yet some are an absolute delight, making one want to savor the menu as much as the meal, while others are simply a few lines on a blackboard. All reflect the style of the place.

Elements of the church year, symbols of faith, representations of current events, or interpretive sayings can be used on the front cover. It is relatively inexpensive to reproduce photographs on bulletin stock. A competent printer, designer, or camera store proprieter can tell you how this can be done. Drawings can be duplicated on a mimeograph, often in more than one color.

Bulletin covers distributed by denominational offices are generally in good taste and provide basic facts about denominational program and identity. If these are used, imagination is needed to supplement the information with local connections and with background on the worship event itself. Some congregations have covers printed showing their building or worship symbol. Although this continuity makes the bulletin a useful tool to send or hand out to a new person, its liability is that the cover is always the same, leading one to dismiss it quickly with the unspoken response, "I've seen that before." Perhaps it would be better to design a handsome brochure, with the church's picture and story on it, to be used with new people and shut-ins. Then, the bulletin can be varied weekly, so that each worshiper is greeted with the image, "This is a new day. These are the elements that will be used to celebrate today."

If you want to utilize a worship innovation, let the bulletin help to interpret it. Unhappily, here's how one church flunked this test: One Sunday the pastor decided to use the kiss of peace in the worship service. The kiss of peace is, after all, an ancient and honorable part of Christian history. But it was new to the congregation; and it was news to the members that it had any history behind it. One Sunday it was something that just happened. Two families left the church as a result, claiming to be offended at having their persons violated with "such indecencies." The church newsletter and the bulletin could have interpreted this custom, and described its historical setting and its rationale for use in this particular service.

Another church has a marvellous way of linking the congregation with the needs of its members. Placed on the chapel altar are cards for people for whom specific prayer requests are made: the bereaved, the ill, those facing crises, those celebrating joyful events or circumstances. During the week, members stop by the chapel, review the cards, and pray individually for these persons. If someone making such a request desires, her or his name appears in the bulletin the following Sunday, and that person becomes the focus of part of the pastoral prayer. Thus, the bulletin plays a part in the prayer chain of that congregation.

Creating the Church's Own Symbol

Many judicatories invite each member congregation to make a banner representing its life and mission, to be displayed when all the churches assemble. It does make a spectacular sight! A number of churches develop symbols, which they use on letterheads, bulletins, and throughout their building.

The creation of a church symbol is not a task to be done quickly and casually. A congregation should give careful attention to such questions as: For whom is the symbol being prepared? Where and how will it be used? What are the key elements out of our life as a people that should be expressed in such a symbol? Why do we want a symbol at this time? Consideration needs to be given to the symbols that already have currency in the congregation.

This task offers a fine opportunity for the creative people in the congregation to use their talents. They can let their aesthetic imaginations soar. The symbol needs to stand the test of time, and one way to be sure about this is to create more than one and to arrange for them to be used on different occasions. Let the congregation live into each of them until the one with long-term durability emerges.

There are several criteria for the "right" symbol:

First, it should encourage growth in imagination and in new meaning. There should be room to grow in it. Meaning and potential should not be exhausted in a single glance.

Second, the symbol should touch the experience of members of the congregation in a special way. It should be "ours." It should feel like "us."

Third, the symbol should provide a link with the Christian tradition and experience.

Fourth, the symbol should involve a balance of nurture and mission. The Christian faith has an internal dimension and an outreach dimension. Somehow the symbol should point in both directions.

One church came up with a round symbol, with intergenerational figures pointing out as spokes to the hub. Their arms are linked, symbolizing caring and community. The final shape of the symbol was decided upon after an open, careful process of input from individuals and groups. The elements to be symbolized were sorted out, and various drawings were rendered. The congregation lived with the choices for awhile, until the current symbol seemed right to most. It now appears on this church's bulletin and newsletter, in newspaper ads, and on posters. In addition, an artist in the church did a bronze casting so that members could have their own copies of this symbol. These make fine gifts for new members and for others.

Sharing the Gifts of Artists. . . . Let the artists among us develop symbols in their chosen forms that express creativity and response to God. Clockwise: Christ statue in bronze, sculptor, Walter Erlebacher; pulpit carvings; cloth banner, St. Andrew's Presbyterian Church, Newport Beach, CA; hands at altar, United Church of Christ, Newaygo, MI.

Sharing the Gifts of Artists

We want to suggest a way to relate the senses, the aesthetic, and the liturgical elements. Most congregations have in their membership or in their community a number of diverse artists—woodworkers, potters, poets, dramatists, metal sculptors, dancers, and painters. Potentially, they are fantastic resources for worship and for community-building, but often their talents are hidden. Bring them out of hiding by having an artists' day. The theme of creativity and our response to the Creator is an exciting one to build around the form of the artist. Focus on the meaning and symbolization of the artists' work.

Artists should not be programmed into stilted religious symbolism. In their search for meaning and the expression of beauty let them develop symbols to celebrate the stuff of life and human experience. Jesus found the metaphors of faith in mustard seeds, a lost coin, grain, and a wayward son. What are the contemporary metaphors of our faith? Let's ask the artists in our midst to show us!

The theatre of the spirit takes place on an environmental stage, which includes surroundings, the senses, the atmosphere, and the cultural/historical context. These factors either enhance or inhibit the possibilities of our worship. Of course, they are not totally subject to our influence, for the Spirit does blow where it will. Yet a great many environmental elements can be shaped to help us achieve the response of the creature to the Eternal and the response to one another that is at the heart of worship.

A Checklist

Here is a checklist to assist worship leaders in preparing space and equipment before a worship service:

ITEM	READY?	COMMENTS
Theme		
Liturgical Materials in Place and Ready for Use		
Symbols		
Bible		
Appropriate Lighting on and in Working Order		
Appropriate Sound on and in Working Order		
Orders of Worship Available		
Candles Lighted		
Pew Envelopes, Pencils, Attendance Forms		
Worship Notes in Place		
Participants Briefed and in Place		
Furniture Properly Arranged		
Musical Items in Readiness		
Windows and Doors Open or Closed as Desired		
Air Conditioning/Heating Properly Adjusted		
Preparatory Objects (Dustcloths, etc.) Out of Sight		
Emergency Procedures (Medical/Fire) Under Control		

The Bible in Worship. . . . As the Bible reflects the dynamic relationship between God and the people of God, it becomes the core book of the worshiping community.

CHAPTER 6

The Bible in Worship

The Bible is both the book of the worshiping community and a terrific worship resource. It reflects the dynamic relationship between God and the people of God. The Bible influences worship in many ways. Here are a few examples: Chapter 2 indicated that the very structure of worship we've chosen comes from Isaiah 6. Hymns draw largely upon biblical material, and a number are paraphrases of psalms. Prayers use biblical metaphors. The material of the church year and of the sacraments relies entirely upon biblical texts. Preaching is preaching of the Word, breaking open contemporary meanings of the ancient book.

The bottom line is that scripture should determine the theme for a worship service. Such elements as hymns, prayers, anthems, and sermon should relate to that theme. Therefore, the Bible becomes the vertebrate structure of the service.

The Bible is not just a book or even a book of books (the Latin word *biblia* means a library). It represents the shared life of the faith community, which entered into the covenant God offered before there was a book. The Bible reflects that community's experience with God and with life. In fact, the word scripture, in its root meaning, is "an act of writing," an act that records events which have already transpired. We come to the book and meet the life it conveys. It is a map of past, shared life experiences that points the direction for the present and the future.

Try this with your congregation or in an adult or youth study group: Ask the members to share how the Bible comes alive for them. In small groups use pencil and paper, discussion and reporting, or art media. We did this once with a group of veteran church workers, many of whom were clergy who were getting ready to teach about resources in "Christian Education: Shared Approaches." We asked them to use various art forms to portray their answers to the question, "How did (does) the Word come alive for you?" Using crayons, paints, pipe cleaners, and paper, they gave their answers. Not one drew a book. No one showed a person in a pulpit or worship-leading position. Each expression was of people in the midst of life; sometimes in crisis, more often in a context of joy and relationships. The Word becomes flesh in the very midst of our own lives.

The Bible is something of a problem for the church. While it is foundational for worship and life, much of it is unknown to many who participate in congregational life. People are not familiar with its idiom and context. Because scripture reading time is often a "ho hum" or "read the bulletin" time, careful attention must be given to making the dramatic links between the biblical world and the lives of your people. Here are some ways to do this:

First, have Bibles in the pews. The Bibles should all be the same version, to make unison or responsive reading possible. Encourage the congregation to read in unison or to follow the reading silently.

Second, explain in advance the context of the particular passage you will read. You may want to point out, as people thumb through the pages with you, chapters that predate and focus the passage of the day. The context should tell who wrote the material, for what purpose, and to what audience. Key words or concepts that are central to the passage and are likely to be unfamiliar should be defined.

Third, use dramatic means to spotlight the reading. For example, in Hungary in the Reformed Church it is customary for the congregation to stand as the preacher announces and reads the sermon text. The standing posture compares with the standing ovation audiences sometimes give to performers. This simple device focuses both preacher and congregation on the biblical foundation. It is a dramatic moment.

Other ways to do it include a choral statement that the congregation sings before and after the reading. In many places it is traditional to have the congregation stand for the reading of the Gospel. One church has two scriptural-type sections in its worship service: one is called "The Ancient Testimony" and is from the Bible; the other is "The Modern Word" and is taken from a contemporary source. The two are correlated and reinforce each other.

A list of biblical passages covering each Sunday in the church year, including some of the special weekday celebrations, is known as a lectionary. When a congregation uses a lectionary that is widely publicized, church members can prepare themselves for the reading of a given day.

Sometimes the arts can be used in creative tension with the scripture. One can use reader's theatre or pantomime, where particular verses or scenes are acted out as they are read. Slides, banners, or special treatment of the altar can be correlated with scripture passages.

Fourth, read well. Often laypersons are asked to read the scripture, even though clergy lead the rest of the service. Sometimes such readers do not have the background and understanding of context or pronunciation; thus, the result is incoherent or dull. Practice in the room where the reading will take place. If you are not doing a unison reading, choose the translation or version that best communicates the intended meaning of a passage. If the congregation is reading with you, it is possible to do a second reading from another version, after the unison reading.

Fifth, watch out for sexism in words, or obscure references that make the passage unintelligible or offensive. Many times sexist references are just bad translations. Also, sometimes the meaning of a word in biblical times is different from present-day usage. Paraphrasing or substituting should be offered in the interest of helping people get to the core of the biblical meaning, not just to be flippant.

How to Use Biblical Material

The contemporary question, "What is the authority of scripture?" need not be overpowering. The word authority has the same root as "author." The author of something is credible to us. We trust the book or the statement because we believe the author is reliable. In the case of the Bible, it is the author of the book who has the authority. Matthew records this experience with Jesus: "When Jesus finished these sayings, the crowds were astonished at his teaching, for he taught them as one who had authority, and not as their scribes [Matt. 7:28-29]." They believed him and they believed in him. He was credible to them. No one or nothing has authority for or over us until we come to believe in that authority. For example, Jesus used homespun examples with which people identified in such a way that they claimed an authority because these examples connected with their experience. Whether the events mentioned in the story of the good Samaritan or the prodigal son actually happened is beside the point; the point is that they explained the meaning of human existence in an authentic way that people understood and believed.

In dealing with a particular biblical passage two words are essential—text and context. Each text has a particular form in its original language. Checking several translations may help us get closer to the original form of the text. Also, each passage was set in a specific time and place. We call this the context. Although it is important to learn what the original context was, keep in mind that context has another meaning—our own present time. When we read a text in our time, we need to understand both the original context and the passage's meaning in the context of our own time and place. Remember that the Bible was written over many centuries; therefore, one part of scripture builds upon another. For instance, the great commandments Jesus gives in Mark 12:29-31 appeared in earlier form in the Old Testament; thus, the Bible had a developing life as the faith community experienced its meaning in the context of their own lives.

For example, Luke 2:14 records the praise of angels at Jesus' birth. The King James Version reads: "Glory to God in the highest, and on earth peace, good will toward men." Checking other translations— the *Revised Standard Version of the Bible*, *The New English Bible*, and *The Jerusalem Bible*—enables us to discover that the most common text is "Glory to God in the highest, and on earth peace among men with whom he is pleased," which involves a more limited number of people. The original context for the passage is a patriarchal one, in which both the beneficiaries and God are described with male pronouns. In our present-day context, in order to get the full meaning of the passage, it is important to translate it, "Glory to God in the highest, and on earth peace among people with whom God is pleased."

Bible tools are available to help with our planning. A concordance (such as *Nelson's Complete Concordance of the Revised Standard Version*[1]) is an alphabetical index listing places in the Bible where principal words appear. *The Interpreter's Dictionary of the Bible*, in four volumes, is similar to any other dictionary, except that its scope is limited to the Bible.[2] *The Interpreter's Bible* is a twelve-volume series that provides background on the text and some ideas about the text's contemporary meaning.[3] There are also multivolume commentaries on the Bible books, such as *The Anchor Bible*.[4]

The fact that "interpreter" is used in several of the above-mentioned book titles reminds us that the Bible does not interpret itself. People use their minds, imagination, and Bible study tools to explore and share its meaning. Actually, there is a whole approach to interpretation, called hermeneutics, that refers to principles of interpretation. We come to understand certain patterns of thought in a given book or throughout the Bible, and this helps us to interpret a given passage. For example, because Paul thought that the end of the world would come in a very short time, much of his teaching and writing is set against this crisis view. This understanding of Paul is a hermeneutical principle that applies throughout his letters.

How do we know which version of the Bible to use? Here is the experience of the First Congregational Church (UCC) in Pasadena, California: This church has a vital, active Bible study group that meets weekly. The pastors choose the scriptures they plan to use at least two weeks ahead of time so the Bible study group can give the passages a thorough review. Various versions of the Bible are consulted to establish the basic text and to understand its meaning. Based upon consideration of the Hebrew-Greek roots as well as contemporary usage, the class agrees on the appropriate translation. Sometimes that means writing one of their own. This version is printed in the bulletin for the appropriate Sunday and becomes the focal point for that day's worship. Thus, scripture reflects the life of the congregation. At the same time, a meaningful and contemporary version of the text is available to all.

Ways to Make the Bible Live

Participatory habits and forms can be developed so that they become the norm in congregational worship. We have already mentioned unison reading of the scripture lesson. The Bible can also be used in litanies and in responsive readings. Here is a sample litany that draws especially upon the witness of women in the Bible and in the church's experience:

Leader: Creator God, hear now our prayer of gratitude and thanksgiving for creation in general, for our creation, and for all creativity. . . . We lift our voices in the Magnificat of Mary:

People: Our souls magnify the Lord, and our spirits rejoice in God our savior.

Leader: That we stand with generations of women who know that the Lord their God is one God; who love the Lord with all their hearts and mind and strength; who established the legacy of Sarah and Deborah and Ruth.

People: Our souls magnify the Lord, and our spirits rejoice in God our savior.

Leader: That we share the news with those first women at the tomb, who went forth to proclaim the gospel of Jesus Christ; who served the early Christians with zeal; who were named Mary and Phoebe and Priscilla.

People: Our souls magnify the Lord, and our spirits rejoice in God our savior.

Leader: That we can remember those women who shaped the church in cloistered community and civil court; who listened to inner voices and pursued mystical union; who mothered and married the "fathers of the faith"; who loved the church when it was most unlovable.

People: Our souls magnify the Lord, and our spirits rejoice in God our savior.

Leader: That we can honor women who defended the reformed faith and supported the reformers; who gave up comforts and family for their convictions; who were sometimes called witches and often became martyrs; who arrived in the new world and took new responsibilities.

People: Our souls magnify the Lord, and our spirits rejoice in God our savior.

Leader: That we now recall those women who came to this land not on the deck, but in the dark hold of a slave ship; who preserved an African heritage and understood the liberating message of the Christian gospel; who nurtured a church under Jim Crow and Daddy Grace; who know the double jeopardy of being black and female.

People: Our souls magnify the Lord, and our spirits rejoice in God our savior.

Leader: That we now listen to those native American sisters, whose people were here long before anyone else came to this country; who remind us of the interrelated fabric of earth and sky and sea; who know the pain of displacement and betrayal; who have much to share with all women.

People: Our souls magnify the Lord, and our spirits rejoice in God our savior.

Leader: That we can read in history of missionaries who heard a call to teach and heal in the name of Jesus; who shared their faith with women and children throughout the world; who exercised authority with charity; who widened the horizons and expanded the vision of the church.

People: Our souls magnify the Lord, and our spirits rejoice in God our savior.

Leader: That we know also of strong women who stayed home and worked in groups and churches to change American life; who founded antislavery societies, Sunday schools, peace movements, suffrage organizations, and temperance halls; who saved and raised monies for mission at home and abroad; who were proud of "women's work" and kept the churches going.

People: Our souls magnify the Lord, and our spirits rejoice in God our savior.

Leader: That we are heirs of women who challenged the status quo and pioneered in new roles; who insisted upon a woman's right to preach the gospel, to practice medicine, to defend the law, to hold public office; who refused to let tradition and custom stifle their gifts; who call the church to accept new forms of leadership today.

People: Our souls magnify the Lord, and our spirits rejoice in God our savior.

Leader: That there are women who have worked in the churches as wives of pastors; who, although too often unacclaimed and unnoticed, have given of themselves in a faithful and dedicated ministry.

People: Our souls magnify the Lord, and our spirits rejoice in God our savior.

Leader: That we are enriched by the influx of Pacific and Asian women who bridge the cultural gulf between East and West and raise our global awareness; who come from islands where women have a valued tradition; who know the problems of multi-cultural and multi-lingual communities in our urban society.

People: Our souls magnify the Lord, and our spirits rejoice in God our savior.

Leader: That we are learning to love those women who are variously called Latino, Hispanic, Chicano, Mexican, and Puerto Rican; who speak Spanish in our church; who know the journeys of employment and the waste of unemployment; who add yet another culture and language to our united church.

People: Our souls magnify the Lord, and our spirits rejoice in God our savior.

Leader: We offer this prayer of thanksgiving and gratitude. We are many and yet we are one. We are members of the church of Jesus Christ. We are empowered for mission because of these women. Thank you, Lord. Amen.[5]

In addition to its being used in litanies, the Bible is expressed in many ways throughout the worship service. Because the scripture becomes the grounding for the message, or sermon, the sermon becomes the preached word, and the Bible is experienced as the book of life.

A hymn can be related to scripture. If you use a hymn-of-the-month pattern, a particular hymn can be linked to one or more related biblical passages so that hymn and Bible reinforce each other.

Dance or dramatic interpretations can be given to biblical material. In the repertoire of classical ballet a number of biblical themes

Ways to Make the Bible Live. . . . Participatory habits and forms such as dramatic interpretations of biblical material can be developed so that they become the norm in congregational worship.

and personalities are re-created, for instance, the creation, the prodigal son, Salome, Joseph, Job, Jesus.

Often one deals more faithfully with the Bible when one is not portraying a biblical character but exploring in dance a biblical theme, such as repentance, forgiveness, love, and grace. The connection with the Bible may need to be made through the reading of a scripture passage while the theme is portrayed in dance. There is often a contrast between biblical content and biblical style.

Plays and musicals like *A Man for All Seasons, J.B., Luther, St. Joan, Jesus Christ Superstar,* and *Godspell* relate directly to biblical material. Selections from such works can be included in worship patterns from time to time.

Many anthems draw heavily from the scriptures. An anthem should be chosen with the text of the service in mind. The words of the anthem, along with the biblical reference it is taken from, can be printed in the bulletin.

Symbols in the church that have a biblical source should be clearly identified in the bulletin and in the newsletter, in teaching programs, and in sermons. Thus, the Bible comes to be seen as a living reference, not just as a book on a stand.

Bible study in youth and in adult classes can be reciprocally related to corporate worship. Those who prepare for the service can consult curriculum materials for correlations. Then the worship experience can have an impact on the classes, and these groups can, in turn, influence both the choice of biblical material and its interpretation.

The Bible and Women

Although the thousand years during which the Bible was written saw vast changes in the human landscape, the culture of the Bible people remained primarily patriarchal. In the face of that patriarchal culture, two remarkable truths emerge—first, that women had a significant place in Israel's life, and second, that God language was never exclusively male. As we seek to be faithful to the biblical context and to the needs of our time, these facts are instructive.

Solely masculine translations are not only inaccurate and distorted, but they tend to limit our understanding of God in another way. Old Testament people thought God to be so awesome that they did not speak the divine name. They simply wrote the letters YHWH. We add the vowels and say Yahweh, or Jehovah, as the King James Version has it. Thus, we need to find ways to describe God with both male and female pronouns and to recover the diverse metaphors the Bible uses to refer to the deity.

Many key words and concepts are feminine in the original Hebrew and Greek. We need to gain a fuller understanding of this in order to help women and men gain a full sense of the richness of the Bible. In the following excerpt from *The Jerusalem Bible*, "wisdom" is treated as a feminine word:

> All that is hidden, all that is plain,
> I have come to know,
> Instructed by Wisdom who designed them all.
>> For within her is a spirit intelligent, holy,
>> unique, manifold, subtle,
>> active, incisive, unsullied,
> irresistible, beneficent, loving to humanity,
> steadfast, dependable, unperturbed,
> almighty, all-surveying
> penetrating all intelligent, pure
> and most subtle spirits;
>> for Wisdom is quicker than any motion;
>> she is so pure, she pervades and permeates all things.
> —Book of Wisdom 7:21-24, JB

As we use the Bible for study, worship, and preaching we give attention to the key actors. An effort should be made to deal with the women in the Bible and to overcome the blind spots of the patriarchal perspective. In the Garden of Eden, Eve is a strong, intelligent character, not just Adam's rib or an afterthought.[6] When we lift up Abraham as the one who journeyed by faith into the unknown, we need to remember that Sarah went too. Isaac was the potential sacrifice of Abraham *and* Sarah. Deborah was a judge in Israel. Queen Esther was a heroine to her people as she saved them from certain destruction. Moses was saved by women, and his sister Miriam led the Hebrew people in dancing and celebration after they had crossed the Red Sea. Ruth broke the ethnic barrier and provided a model for intergenerational friendship between two caring women. Mary, Jesus' mother, is a central figure throughout the Gospel stories. Mary Magdalene was a strong, faithful friend of Jesus'. Women such as Phoebe and Priscilla were key leaders in the New Testament church.

The Bible is a book of great richness that enhances our understanding of worship and of life. To understand its feminine side is to enlarge its promise for us all.

This chapter emphasizes two points: First, the Bible is the source of our liturgy, our work as a people. It gives shape to our worship and is a deep wellspring out of which to draw rich understandings and metaphors of faith. Second, the Bible is a living book. It is the book of a people and their day-to-day life. It is our book. Through its revealing pages we understand our life in fresh ways. To find this life involves a continuing reworking of our understanding of the Bible—its text, context, world, and meaning. Such a search is at the heart of the theatre of the spirit.

Music in Worship. . . . "Sing psalms and hymns and spiritual songs with thankfulness in your hearts."

CHAPTER 7

Music in Worship

Paul tells the Colossians that Christians are to "sing psalms and hymns and spiritual songs with thankfulness in your hearts to God [3:16]." Psalms have been part of the said and sung worship of the Jewish community since before Jesus' time. Early in its life, Christian worship included musical components. The Gregorian chant, which was part of the liturgy in the early Middle Ages, became a dominant foundation of the Western music tradition. During the Renaissance the great composers wrote music for the church. Luther understood that to give the church back to the laity meant freeing their voices and spirits to sing, so he wrote several dozen hymns himself, often rescuing a tune from the tavern or the street. Calvin and his followers in Old and New England used the psalm tune as their musical mode in worship.

The chorale, given form by both Luther and Bach, came to America from Germany, especially with the Lutheran migrations. The Wesleys brought music with them, and the Wesleyan movement was a singing tradition in settled town and on the frontier. The Puritan tradition in America lined hymns, meaning the leader sang a line and then the congregation repeated it. The harpsicord, piano, and organ, as well as strings, winds, and brass, were used early in American life by both Protestants and Catholics for the praise of God.

Like movement and language, music is a mode of expression and meaning. Psalm 150 is an invitation to praise God with

> fanfares on the trumpet,
> . . . upon lute and harp;
> . . . with tambourines and dancing,
> . . . with flute and strings,
> . . . with the clash of cymbals,
> . . . with triumphant cymbals . . . [3–5, NEB]

Sometimes we are on the receiving end and savor meanings that are communicated by the choir and organ; and sometimes we are on the giving end, as we express ourselves in our special offering of music. Individually and together, through music we express who we are, what we believe, and how we intend to pursue God's mission. Music conveys the full range of moods of the human spirit. A lyricist or a composer shares with us through words and/or music his or her vision of the faith. Choir, organist, and congregation express in their own ways their sense of the meaning of an anthem or a hymn.

Music has an integrity of its own as a language and as a communication form. It is a medium we have available, and like any other medium, it has its own forms and disciplines. Music is an important language for faith to learn to speak, so careful planning for its role in worship is essential. Music in worship is to be enjoyed for its own sake and as a means of celebrating the presence of God.

Music in worship performs several functions: It is a form of offering in its own right. Artist, performer, and congregational singer alike use their gifts of musical expression as a response to God. John Wesley described our offering through hymns with these admonitions:

Learn the tunes.
Sing them as printed.
Sing *all* . . . Let not a slight degree of weakness or weariness hinder you. If it is a cross to you, take it up, and you will find it a blessing.
Sing *lustily* and with a good courage.
Beware of singing as if you are half dead, or half asleep, but lift up your voice with strength. Be no more afraid of your voice now, nor more ashamed of its being heard, than when you sing the songs of *Satan*.
Sing *modestly*. Do not bawl . . . strive to unite your voices together so as to make one clear melodious sound.
Sing in *time*. Do not run before or stay behind . . . and take care not to sing too slow. . . .
Above all, sing *spiritually*. Have an eye to God in every word you sing. Aim at pleasing [God] more than yourself, or any other creature. In order to do this, attend strictly to the sense of what you sing, and see that your heart is not carried away with the sound, but offered to God continually.[1]

Music complements the service's movement and its oral and silent parts. It is not a filler or a breather or a decoration, although we must ask whether, in fact, these words describe the level to which music in our congregation has descended. Its contrast with the spoken word and the silent moments is pleasing to the soul and enhancing to our aesthetic sense.

Moreover, music's variations in worship are remarkably diverse. Music has its own congregational forms in hymns, responses, the Gloria Patri, the Doxology, and antiphonal patterns. Music has its choral forms in calls to worship, introits, anthems, and responses. Music has its individual forms, like the cantor or the tenor soloist. Music has its ensemble forms, as combinations of singers and instrumentalists present musical selections. Music has its instrumental forms, like the prelude, the offertory, and the postlude.

A variety of instruments can be used in the praise of God: a flute is extraordinary; yet, trumpets on an Easter alleluia are breathtaking. The organ is wondrously complex and spirited, capable of full, deep chords that seem to reach the spinal chord, or the tiniest echo, that makes us hold our breaths. A guitar or an autoharp undergirds and complements singing in moving ways. Even recorded music can be effective when used thoughtfully.

Types of music can be as varied as the human voice and imagination. Music for the church is Bach, Beethoven, Brahms, Mozart, and Verdi. It is also Bernstein, Brubeck, the Beatles, the Beach Boys, and the Bee Gees. The traditions of plainsong, the chorale, the psalm tune, the revival hymn, the strident songs of the social gospel, and contemporary nonsexist hymns are all part of music's response and resources for worship. Music beautifully expresses worship's moods—its sense of the solitary and of solidarity; the elements of awe, confession, acceptance, and response; and the human spirit's heights and depths.

There is a marvellous story—perhaps apocryphal—of a member of the audience who came up to George Frederick Handel after a performance of *The Messiah*. He told Handel how much he had enjoyed the music. "I am sorry," the composer is reported to have said. "I had wished to make you a better person through my music." Music has that capacity!

Music touches our moods and our spirits in unique ways. When our defenses prevent us from being in touch with our own deep feelings, often music can break through and open a new world to us. It is an acceptable and effective medium or catalyst to get us in touch with our own spirit. This is true whether we are performer or listener.

Music helps us build community. Together we express and experience the power of a spiritual or a chorale. We all know the tune, and there is solidarity in that. It is enlightening to visit other churches and cultures, and discover the universality of music.

Music is highly participatory. Even when we are part of an audience, the elements of sight, sound, rhythm, and bodily movement come into play. We smile, cry, hum, sway, and tap our feet. If we're not too inhibited, we click our fingers or clap. In addition to formal worship occasions, we participate in music's ministry in camps, intergenerational groups, family events, and fellowship occasions.

A musical program has its own validity as a component of the congregation's worship life, along with some good side effects. Musical groups provide a place of participation for lots of people who are not attracted by other elements of the church. This type of program is also a resource for membership, both attracting choir members and drawing people to the congregation who want good music to be part of their worship experience.

Guidelines for Music Planning in Worship

Do not let music be an afterthought in worship planning. It becomes an afterthought if it follows all other planning or if it is treated casually. Music has its own quality of life as an element of worship, and that resource is an essential part of worship planning.

As you do your music planning, first of all, *start with yourself* and your sense of what music is and can be. One's voice and body are God-given instruments; ears and intuition are resources for hearing and perceiving music. As a worship planner, you should believe in what you're doing with the music you use. Your energy, imagination, and commitment are on the line.

Size and scope should be given consideration. Use your imagination to enlarge the possibilities. At the same time be realistic about what is possible and appropriate. Grant Spradling says,

> I wonder if we need to be concerned that so much of what we provide
> and the expectations we encourage in small churches causes a longing
> for "big church" kinds of worship. We need to find those resources
> that are appropriate for small churches with very limited resources of
> materials and sophistication. Autoharps, pianos, and unison music
> can be far superior to poorly performed cut versions of Bach, Vivaldi,
> and electronic organ recitals.[2]

Second, *plan long range* for musical expression. This involves making it somebody's business to provide personnel and budget and to build the library and repertoire. Convene intentional worship planning meetings to establish clear goals for each service, each season, and each year; make arrangements to implement the goals and themes.

Some issues requiring immediate attention include places to rehearse and to store music and such equipment as music stands and music folders. A place to hang robes is also needed, and provisions must be made for their care. Check lighting and sound arrangements for both performing and rehearsal space. Plan how to meet any deficiencies in these areas.

One needs to plan carefully how the various musical elements—choir(s), instrumentalists, dancers, organist, and choir director—will be housed. Where will they sit? Where will they perform? How will they get there? If you have a divided chancel, special consideration should be given to the placement of the choir. If the choir is small, have everyone sit on one side. If both sides are used, try having all four parts on each side or move to the center to perform.

There are logistical matters to consider as well. When will various groups rehearse during the week and on Sunday morning? What time will the choir be called to be ready for the services? If there are two services, how will choral music be provided for both?

Give careful attention to long-range budget and personnel questions. You may be in good shape for this Sunday or season but with no reserves the long-range prognosis may be courting disaster. Build a financial reserve, and initiate a talent development scheme so there is a talent reserve.

Third, gear the music to the *rhythm of worship*. Prelude, hymn, and introit should convey a sense of awe, wonder, and mystery of the holy. Response, anthem, and hymn should express not-yet-ness and penitence. A sung statement of faith, response, and hymn should symbolize acceptance. Offertory, response, hymn, and postlude should signal dedication and offering. Music can undergird the liturgy's flow through the elements. In addition, it can express each in its unique language.

Fourth, music should be *integrated with the church year*. Because the meaning of a season can be reflected musically in ways the spoken or symbolic word cannot touch, select music appropriate to the season. The Christmas portions of *The Messiah*, Christmas carols, "O Sacred Head, Now Wounded," "Let Us Break Bread Together on Our Knees," and "Christ the Lord Is Risen Today" are examples of themed music. Tunes and texts from other times and cultures can also be introduced.

Fifth, all planning for worship needs to be *wholistic*. The entire worship leadership needs to plan together so that environment, style, form, elements, and leadership can be seen as they relate to one another. Specifically, music should enhance the spoken word and vice versa.

Sixth, make sure that the *music doesn't sound all the same*. Diversity of sound can be achieved by varying the mood and type of selections in the repertoire, by using different vocal combinations—ensembles, solos, duets, men's voices, women's voices—and through the use of various instrumental ensembles. Balance and variety are needed within a service and within a season. Plan the layout and flow of the service with attention to the variety of sounds available for the praise of God and the enjoyment of people. If the hymns are rousing, maybe a poignant anthem should be chosen. If the anthem is stirring or strident, the hymns may need to be devotional and introspective.

Seventh, as you plan for music, fix upon a *mixture of consistency and experimentation* or growth. It is essential for every congregation to know the fixed points in a service or a season and what it can count on. At the same time, every congregation should venture into new territory. "Sing to [the Lord] a new song," the psalmist directs us in Psalm 33:3.

Eighth, *trust gut and artist!* The right music will probably be what feels right to you and to the others who are planning it. A musician is an artist, and it is the artist's gift to use his or her craft to express meaning.

Musical Elements in Worship

An *organ* or a *piano* is often used to gather and to dismiss people; to accompany hymns, anthems, and responses; and to provide transitions between worship elements. But don't forget that they are instruments to be listened to in their own right. Many times the organ is a church's pride and joy, and the celebration of its musical possibilities provides some great moments in a church's life.

If you are starting fresh in securing an instrument, look carefully at your church's physical layout—size of the sanctuary; potential space for pipes; arrangement of choir, pulpit, congregation; elements of sound and light. Shop around. Find out what churches with similar worship conditions are doing. On what bases have they made their decisions? Are they happy with the results? Talk with dealers and manufacturers' representatives, but also confer with a variety of musicians, instrument builders, and clergy. Discover how they have analyzed and solved their problems. Buy for the long haul, so that you have maximum quality and flexibility. And remember that maintenance is a crucial matter.

A good organist and/or pianist is usually hard to find, and money will certainly be the key issue. Good music is an expense; therefore, careful financial planning and fund raising is essential. Sometimes individuals or groups endow the maintenance of an organ or part of the cost of a musician. Offerings received at organ concerts also help the music budget. Patrons or sponsors who are willing to give $50 or $100 yearly can generally be found. Use your imagination to raise funds. This activity can be fun, and the results are important to a lot of people. Since one tends to get what one pays for, it is necessary to solve any budget problems when planning the musical year.

In looking for an organist or a pianist, consult local musicians. They themselves may be interested in a full- or part-time job, or they may know of musicians who are available. The American Guild of Organists can put you in touch with guild members in your area.[3] Try running an ad in a local or a college newspaper, and in state and national music and religious journals. If you have a good instrument, arrangements can usually be made for someone to teach on it, so that budding organists or pianists can be nurtured, thus providing a solid resource for the congregation's musical program.

The *choir* is a valuable resource in most congregations. Because choir members are volunteers who give their energy, spirit, time, and musicality, they deserve competent direction and encouragement to develop their gifts fully. Even though choristers are volunteers, they can be expected to invest their time, learn the music, and increase their musical ability. Further, their volunteer status is no rationale for sloppiness or low standards. A singer should engage voice and body as he or she reaches for the full potential of the music. A lethargic, uninspired, disinterested choir provides lethargic, uninspired, disinterested worship. Responses or anthems that cannot be understood due to poor diction are shoddy musicianship and an unworthy offering. Your musical director needs to be well organized, competent in music, and able to inspire and discipline a group of people.

What keeps a choir going? Certainly, tradition and loyalty, but what else? How about challenging music, a sense of growth, a sense of excellence, fellowship with other singers, an opportunity to be worthwhile, and positive feedback and encouragement from the congregation? Feedback doesn't mean saying, "Everything was great!" but rather, taking the choir and its music seriously enough to respond affirmatively, critically, and encouragingly.

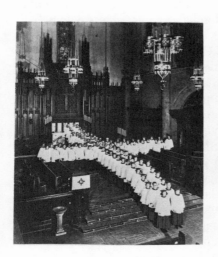

Musical Elements in Worship. . . . . Choirs are volunteers of all ages whose gifts are energy, spirit, time, and musicality. They deserve the best help in developing and presenting these gifts.

A choir needs to develop a basic repertoire that includes selections for each segment of the church year, some old standbys, and a mixture of the classic and the contemporary. Worship leaders and choir directors should research the background of pieces to be sung, so that the choir can express the music's meanings with the fullest knowledge of their potential.

Choirs are available to perform at different kinds of functions. If they are singing a major work, such as Verdi's *Requiem* or Haydn's *Creation*, in a worship setting, attention should be given to the elements of adoration, confession, acceptance, and response. If a performance of this caliber is being given in a concert setting, accurate program notes will help the audience to understand the liturgical message of the work. Various ensembles are able to present a program in worship and in concert settings. On occasion, a church talent night, combined with a potluck supper and a hymnsing, lets everybody get into the act.

Decisions about whether or not to garb choir, organist, and soloists and, if so, how, should be made with a number of factors in mind, for instance, color and style should reflect the sanctuary and be consistent with liturgical colors. Durability and cost are other elements to be considered. Make vestment determinations with all the worship participants in mind: clergy, liturgists, organist, choir, and acolytes. Robes need tender, loving care, including a place to be hung and periodic pressings and repair. A choir that feels well dressed sings proudly.

The choir has a modeling function. Its knowledge of the flow of elements in the worship service enables it to help the congregation to know what's next. The choir is onstage during the entire service, and its energy level needs to remain high. Too often a choir perceives its purpose to be entertaining the congregation rather than singing to the glory of God and facilitating the worship of others. Purposeful movement and positioning can do much to improve the effectiveness of worship, so don't glue the choir to the same spot in the sanctuary.

The role of the *children's choir* is fourfold: educational, musical, liturgical, and social. The *educational* function is probably paramount, due to the inexperience of the children and the large musical world awaiting their exploration. The mode should be one of discovery and excitement, like explorers in unmapped territory. The background of music, composers, and liturgy should be shared with these young choir members, usually in small doses and as it relates to what they are singing.

The children's choir in the church may be the first *musical* experience these children have had with either voice training or choral work; therefore, they deserve your best effort. They should receive instruction in breathing, listening, watching, diction, control, and energy. Since body language is important in singing and children's natural instincts can be utilized, try incorporating some movement to assist them in entering the mood, range, and meaning of the piece of music.

For many children who sing in the choir this will be the first time they will be exposed, in a systematic way, to the *liturgy*. Hopefully, they experience the thrill of adoration, the seriousness of confession, the relief of acceptance, and the urgency of response. Children can find meaning in worship, because these moods are part of their everyday life experience.

The *social* role of a choir for children is significant. Except for certain play functions, a number of children's activities are individualistic. Here you are dealing with an ensemble in which each person counts but in which one part needs to blend with the whole. The discipline and thrill of that experience is important. A choir can be good fun for children and can give them a positive taste of the fellowship dimension of the church's life.

Children's choirs have to build their own repertoires, with the church year and the moods of the spirit in mind. Pieces should be within their voice range and level of accomplishment. As they become conscious of their roles as worship leaders and interpreters of music's meaning, children tend to transcend the negative factors in their cuteness and lack of experience.

Youth choirs hold a lot of promise for churches. Many young people can be reached through this activity, when no other parts of the church's life appeal to them. For others, the youth choir is a wonderful place to accomplish a goal with friends. The moods of the spirit reflected in the fourfold rhythm and in the church year's seasons ring true to young people. They know these moods and seasons; they care about who wrote something and why. With the right kind of leadership, they have the capacity to develop a skilled musical ensemble that is energetic, disciplined, and excellent.

There are many dimensions to the role of youth in music and to the participation of a youth choir in a congregation's life. The choir, of course, sings an occasional service. Sometimes they may carry the whole service. Often a youth choir presents a special performance, or it is the nucleus for a production such as *Godspell*. These musical presentations contribute to the church's youth program by providing musical leadership and by drawing upon the skills of other youth as designers of stage sets, costumers, or instrumental musicians.

A good youth choir pays attention to both the big and the little pictures. It is a highly visible group and needs to be a model of worship excellence. There is leadership responsibility here. Youth need specific instructions—"Be energetic; let your bodies express what the words and music mean; be 'onstage' and present the whole time; no gum chewing; no passing notes, talking, or giggling."

There is a "high" for youth in the dynamics of preparation and performance. The anxiety of getting ready is intense. The sense of knowing you are ready is a unique feeling. The joy of doing something of consequence well; the sense of being part of an ensemble that transcends collective individualities; the interplay of congregation and choir—these kinds of experiences cannot be replaced for young people or for anyone else. If there is no youth choir in your church, encourage those of high school and college-age to sing in the adult choir.

A rapidly growing church music phenomenon is the bell choir, a precision team that produces an extremely pleasing sound. Under careful direction, the bells can be handled by older children and by youth. The bell choir can be a natural intergenerational possibility as well as an adult musical expression.

Good congregational singing does not just happen. It is necessary for the congregation to receive encouragement, direction, and assistance from the pastor, the choir director, and other worship leaders. The choir can help by knowing and leading the hymns. An organist or pianist who can accompany aggressively and play a singable tempo is a must. Attention must be given to patterns of sound amplification, so that the pastor's voice is not the only one heard. From time to time special practice sessions, like potluck sing-alongs, may be worthwhile to help the congregation achieve its full singing potential. To help learn and value new hymns, try choosing a hymn-of-the-month, to be sung each Sunday for one month. This will increase the congregation's repertoire.

Many churches seem to think that instrumental music means an organ and an occasional Easter trumpet. To the contrary, many choices exist. At one time a number of churches had orchestras, which they felt were "standard equipment"; some churches still have and use them in church and church school. Others use instrumental music occasionally. This can be a part-time timpani, guitar, or flute for a particular service or season; or it can be a full-time guitar, to lead or augment the singing. There may even be a combo to play a folk mass. The diversity is significant. Each instrument and piece has its own integrity, and in its own special way expresses music's gifts and meaning. If you are using professional musicians, be prepared to deal with contract and union matters.

Hymns and Hymnody

A hymn is a religious poem set to music. It is written to be sung by a congregation. The mating of hymn and tune can be started from either direction: sometimes the lyrics are written or chosen and then an appropriate tune is sought; at other times a tune begs for a text to give it vocal expression.

Spend some time with the hymnal and other musical material to be used. Note the book's organization; many hymnals are geared to themes and to seasons of the Christian year. Examine the indexes—composers, authors, first lines, scriptural references—and discover their features. This familiarity makes the book easier to work with, especially when quick decisions have to be made.

There are some things to note about a hymn. Its title is almost always the same as the first line. The name of the hymn tune is usually found under the title and to the right, along with the composer's name and the date of composition. The name of the author and/or translator of the lyrics and the date when the words were written appear on the left, under the title. The numbers or letters following the hymn tune tell how many syllables there are in each line. The abbreviation *LM* stands for long meter, which means eight syllables to each line. *SM* means short meter—the 6.6.8.6 pattern—indicating that the first two lines have six syllables, the third has eight, and the fourth has six. *CM* represents common meter, which is 8.6.8.6.

These syllable patterns are important in teaching and in learning hymns, as well as in matching tunes and texts. For example, "Love Divine, All Loves Excelling" and "Joyful, Joyful, We Adore Thee" are both sung to tunes that are listed as 8.7.8.7.D. This means that the first line has eight syllables, the second seven, and so on. The *D* means that the 8.7.8.7. pattern is doubled. While "Love Divine" is usually sung to the tune called "Beecher," it could also be sung to Beethoven's "Hymn to Joy," which we usually associate with "Joyful, Joyful, We Adore Thee." We know this exchange will work because the syllable pattern is an exact fit. We can use this technique both in composing new words for tunes (or vice versa) or for mating extant tunes and texts.

The signature ($\frac{4}{4}$ or $\frac{3}{4}$) tells the number of beats to the measure. Tunes used for the processional or the recessional should be in $\frac{4}{4}$ time or its equivalent.

Some hymns, because of the mood they convey or their words, belong at the beginning or at the end of the service. Others express the mood of penitence or of affirmation and are appropriate at segments that come in the middle of the service.

Here are some guidelines for hymn selection:

First, the chosen hymn should contribute to the overall theme of the day or event. It should fit its slot and enhance the mood and meaning of the rhythm.

Second, the hymn's theological ideas should be expressive of the faith intentions of the congregation. Does it say what this congregation believes?

Third, the aesthetic qualities of the hymn should pass the muster. It should be a good poem, mated with a well-constructed tune.

Fourth, the tune should be singable. Singability may refer to range or rhythm of the piece, or to the peculiarities of a given congregation, or both. Since there are probably a number of persons in the congregation who do not read the black dots, the hymn tune should be easily remembered or learned. A congregation needs to build its repertoire of hymn favorites, including those that are homemade.

In choosing hymns for children, some other criteria apply: Are the words understandable, and do they have meaning for children? Are the ideas in the lyrics ones you want to communicate to children? Is the tune within the range of their voices? Do text and tune together convey the meanings intended, as used in particular worship context? Actually, these questions probably apply when choosing hymns for any age group.

There are many sources of new hymns; for example: The Hymn Society of America, which occasionally publishes collections of new hymns[4]; lyricists and composers such as Richard Avery and Donald Marsh, who provide collections of quality hymns;[5] and talented congregational members, who should be encouraged to write hymns. In the pew a worshiper needs a good hymnal, supplemented by contemporary selections. These supplementary hymns can be bound in a loose-leaf notebook that can be placed in the pew rack.

If one takes the project seriously and has a little poetry in the soul, it is not difficult to change words of hymns. Hymns and responses can be reworked by substituting a word with the same number of syllables; for example, for "he" we can say "we" or "who"; for "Father" we can use "Maker," "Parent," or "Spirit"; for "Lord" or

"King" we can use "God," "Source," "Light," "Hope," "Love," or "Peace"; and for "man" or "men" we can use "folk," "all," "we," or "one."

Here is the text of "In Christ There Is No East or West."

> In Christ there is no East or West,
> In him no South or North;
> But one great fellowship of love
> Throughout the whole wide earth.
>
> In him shall true hearts everywhere
> Their high communion find;
> His service is the golden cord
> Close-binding all mankind.
>
> Join hands, then, brothers of the faith,
> Whate'er your race may be!
> Who serves my Father as a son
> Is surely kin to me.
>
> In Christ now meet both East and West,
> In him meet South and North;
> All Christly souls are one in him
> Throughout the whole wide earth.[6]

In order to make this favorite old hymn inclusive, before singing it you might suggest to the congregation the following word changes:
Stanza 2, last phrase:

> His spirit is the golden cord
> Close-binding humankind.

Stanza 3:

> Join hands, then, people of the faith,
> Whate'er your status be!
> Who ministers to God's fam'ly
> Is surely kin to me.

Stanza 4, last phrase:

> All Christ-like souls are joined as one
> Throughout the whole wide earth.

In addition to matters dealing with sexism in language and the search for inclusiveness, other concerns can be addressed in hymn rewriting. For example, if we don't want to perpetuate the "up there" notion of God, Grace Moore's reworking of "Be Thou My Vision" serves as a good illustration of how to solve the problem:

Do be my vision,
O God of my heart;
Be to me all in all
And ne'er depart.
You my best thought,
By day or by night,
Waking or sleeping,
Your presence my light.

Do be my wisdom,
And be my abode;
I ever with you
And you with me, God;
You my great Parent,
I your true child;
You in me dwelling,
I with you plied.

Riches I heed not,
Nor one's empty praise,
You my inheritance,
Now and always;
You and you only,
First in my heart,
Eternal Spirit,
Great wealth from the start.

Eternal Spirit,
All praise be to you,
May I find your presence
Bask in the view!
Heart of my own heart,
Whatever befall,
Still be my vision,
Creator of all.[7]

A translation of the familiar Thomas Ken Doxology goes like this:

Praise God from whom all blessings flow;
Praise God, all creatures here below;
Praise God above, ye heavenly host;
Praise God and Christ and Holy Ghost.

A paraphrase of the first phrase of the Gloria Patria uses these words: "Glory be to the Creator, and to the Christ, and to the Holy Ghost."

New material that includes both alternate words and new hymns can be found in such collections as *Because We Are One People, The Shalom Hymnal, Sing Shalom,* and *Sisters and Brothers Sing.*[8] In a number of churches one or more of these collections are placed in the pew racks along with the standard hymnal. Another pattern is to print words to new hymns in the bulletin. If you do use the bulletin method, remember that worshipers will not have the music before them, so use a familiar tune!

Music and Worship Leaders

The worship leadership of a church must see itself as part of a worship planning team whose members complement one another. However, some key questions need to be settled at the outset: Who is ultimately responsible for what in each service of worship? If there is a dispute, whose tastes will prevail? Who will work together in service planning and in establishing priorities? Who will contact and rehearse lay participants? What is the role, function, and authority of the church council, the music committee, and/or the worship committee?

If you are a *pastor,* here are some comments for you: Take as full a measure as you can of your own musical interests and skills, and remember that it is not necessary for you to know everything. But it is important for you to know your strengths and use them, and to know your weaknesses and get help in overcoming them. You may not have had specialized music training, and that is all right, as long as you let those who have help you. You and your congregation deserve the fullest musical expression possible in worship, which means you need to give the same sustained attention to the musical components that you give to the sermon, the prayers, and the order of service.

If a professional musician or musicians, or a team of volunteers shares the leadership with you, be supportive of them. Be glad if they have good ideas. Feel free to seek their counsel on the worship elements for which you have primary responsibility. The worship will be richer and the teamwork more fun if team members feel appreciated as they bring the gifts of their discipline and experience to the planning.

If you are a *professional musician,* please note the emphases on the integrity of the musical components and the importance of team effort. You have special gifts to bring, and that may be difficult for you at times. You may feel that neither the pastor nor the lay members appreciate your insights or the results of your specialized training—and you may be right. If they are not experienced enough to know how to use your expertise, help them with comments like, "There is an awkward spot in the service I could cover," or, "Did you know Ralph Vaughan Williams has a marvellous tune that would be right for this theme?" If your taste and theirs do not mesh, try some "equal time" to help enlarge the areas of mutuality ("I'd like you to consider this Bach tune, and of course, we'll use 'Everybody Rejoice' from *The Wiz*"). If your colleagues feel that you are not interested in enhancing the chosen theme, try saying, "I have a terrific anthem I'd like to use for Palm Sunday. Please look it over, and let's figure out how it can relate to your prayers and sermon."

You have a right to expect the church to treat you as a professional and to support the development of your craft, but most congregations need help in knowing how to do that. You can further your own musical cause a lot by using the bulletin, the newsletter, or program notes to give background on music. It is not unusual for professional musicians in churches to write columns in their churches' newsletter interpreting their work and musical offerings.

If you are a *volunteer music leader*, please realize that the comments about musical integrity and team planning are intended for you too. You may have had professional training and are working in a church that can't afford to pay you. If that is your situation, you should still insist on being treated as a professional.

If being a volunteer means that your training and experience are limited, build upon your strengths. Use your gifts in ways that complement and undergird the worship resources of the pastor and other worship leaders. Be willing to be vulnerable; seek suggestions for your own development and offer suggestions to other team members. Try to get more training along the way. Hopefully, your church can help you do this. Share creatively in your congregation's worship planning.

It is a good idea for the members of the team, pastor and church musicians alike, to attend training conferences together. This builds confidence, competence, and mutuality. In addition, each member of the team should maintain memberships in professional organizations that provide growth, enrichment, and new ideas.

Where to Get Help

A variety of places give assistance in planning for music in worship. Interview organists and choir directors from neighboring churches, or call upon music teachers in public or private schools for help in solving the problems you're facing. "Unions" of music people—

such as state music educators, the American Guild of Organists, or the Choristers' Guild—can aid you in finding helpers, in suggesting sources of music, or in performing music in new ways.

When seeking new music, reach out widely. Consult your denominational bookstore. Pay attention to what's being played on the radio and on television, and list the tunes you like. Visit the library—many of them have publishers' catalogs, background books, and records to borrow. Your neighborhood record store has a listing of albums still available and can point you in helpful directions. Get together with others and trade ideas. Even the best church musicians are constantly taking additional training, seeking new music sources, and trading ideas with one another. Join them!

Most hymnals have a companion volume that gives background information on hymns. An excellent one is *A Guide to the Pilgrim Hymnal,* by Albert C. Ronander and Ethel K. Porter.[9] H. Augustine Smith's *Lyric Religion* tells the story of many hymns.[10]

Many church organizations or entrepreneurs conduct music workshops for both professional and amateur musicians. A local council of churches generally knows where to get information about these. Some addresses are: Proclamation Productions, Inc. (Richard Avery and Donald Marsh), Orange Square, Port Jervis, New York 12771; Choristers' Guild, P.O. Box 38188, Dallas, Texas 75238; American Guild of Organists, 630 Fifth Avenue, New York, New York 10020; *Journal of Church Music,* Fortress Press, 2900 Queen Lane, Philadelphia, Pennsylvania 19129.

A majority of congregations have a music committee that is responsible for hiring personnel, creating a budget, fund raising, planning music events, keeping a library, purchasing and caring for robes, and evaluating the overall music program in the church. The members of this committee have to be advocates for the validity of music in the congregation's life. They are the music lobby and the source of resident imagination concerning new possibilities for music and musicians. They need to be folk who love music and who are determined to make sure it happens and keeps happening. They need to take their job seriously, rise above petty squabbles, and impact the total life of the church. All age and interest groups should be represented. Conversely, the committee should figure out ways to impact all age groups and interests.

The Sound of Music

Serious attention must be paid to the amplification of music. The public address system in many churches is geared to the spoken form of the pulpit and the lectern, which does little to enhance the sound of music. Be sure that the podium microphones have on/off switches so they can be turned off during congregational singing. That way no one voice is dominant.

In developing sound treatments for music, consider all the items that need amplification, such as choir, organ, instrumentals, tapes, and records. John Foley talks about one of these elements:

> One of our major uses for the amplification system has been to "mike" [microphone] the choir, an unorthodox practice with several key advantages. For one thing, an amateur choir may not be able to sing loudly enough to be heard by an entire church, especially if the people are to sing along at times, as well as just listen. But more, we found that the loudspeakers brought the choir sound right into the congregation itself, making it easier for individuals to join in. We put both men and women from the choir on any melody that we want the people to sing with, and have thus created the beginnings of a congregation sound even before the people have begun to join in. With the beginning inertia overcome, it is much easier for individuals in the church to sing along since both men and women can be heard already singing. We also add a soprano harmony and sometimes one for basses to add fulness.[11]

You will need to consider where speakers should be placed to avoid feedback, what kind of equipment is available for the hard of hearing, what kind of amplifiers are needed, where the available power is and needs to be, how cables can be kept from view and out of traffic patterns, how many controls are needed for the system and where they should be located, and where equipment can be safely stored when not in use.

Again, shop around to see what churches that face similar problems have done. Secure the services of a professional sound engineer—not a building contractor with a little sound experience.

Equipment to do what needs to be done is available. It is only a matter of finding the right components and paying for them. If you have a Cadillac building, don't install a Pinto sound system. A good system, if properly taken care of, will last for many years; it is best to put the new equipment under a maintenance contract at the time of purchase. Two tips: don't let hobbyists fool with expensive sound equipment, and be sure your insurance covers the replacement cost of the sound system.

Amplification is not the only issue to consider when dealing with the sound of music. After all, the system only magnifies what is; it does not create. God gave us an incredible range of musical sounds, and we need to use our imaginations to express their fullness. Too often choir directors seem to think that choirs can only sing like an army—in forte and in four parts! Sometimes a choir should try to sing like a flute or a bell or in unison.

Copyright

Under the U.S. copyright law, copyright owners have the exclusive right to print, publish, copy, and sell their protected works. Under the copyright law that became effective January 1, 1978 the copyright on a work published after that date is in effect for the author's life plus fifty years. Works published in the United States prior to September 1, 1906 are in the public domain. Works copyrighted between January 1, 1950 and December 31, 1977 are protected for twenty-eight years, and the copyright may be renewed for forty-seven years. Works copyrighted between the 1906 and 1950 dates were protected for twenty-eight years; if the copyright was renewed, the renewal has automatically been extended to a total term of seventy-five years from the original copyright date.[12]

Effective long-range planning of music and worship allows adequate time to secure needed music and to arrange for permission to duplicate copyrighted material. Sometimes it is difficult to tell who owns the copyright on a given piece of material; however, the publisher of this work can probably supply this information. When requesting permission, state what you want to use and give its source, list any modifications you plan to make, and specify in what context the material is to be used.

Your local library can be helpful in providing data on copyright law and practice, and in furnishing the addresses of publishers you may need to contact. For further information, write to the United States Copyright Office, Library of Congress, Washington, D.C. 20559.

Two adaptations may apply to your situation: The new copyright law provides for an educational purpose reproduction of copyrighted material, and most publishers have designated a maximum number of words that may be quoted without their permission.

If you do secure permission to quote a copyrighted work, be sure to credit the material according to the publisher's or author's requested form of identification.

Celebrating Music's Place. . . . Musical happenings provide variety and offer unique insights into the meaning of worship and the Christian faith.

Celebrating Music's Place

Part of worship planning is providing occasions when choirs, organists, and music leaders are recognized for the gifts they share. This should be done frequently from the pulpit and also in the bulletin or newsletter. It can be done through special services or celebrations. Beth Knight says that choir members and church school teachers are

> the most forgotten volunteers in the church. How about an annual banquet or dessert night or special program to honor them with certificates or other mementos? Or perhaps a special coffee hour where these volunteers wear tags or big, bold signs that say they serve their church in such a consistent, important way.[13]

The worship calendar should be planned in such a way that the choir and organist take full responsibility for one or two services each year. Musical happenings provide variety and offer unique insights into the meaning of worship and the Christian faith. Choir members see the results of their work, and they are lifted beyond themselves so as to reach many people in deeply significant ways.

One church recognized the importance of the choral contribution and used a litany of dedication to say so:

Leader:	David brought the Ark of the Lord into Jerusalem with trumpets and dancing.
Choirs:	We use our gifts to express our faith vigorously.
Leader:	In the psalms we are told to sing before our God with dignity.
Choirs:	Through music we enter into tradition.
Leader:	The psalms joyfully proclaim the spiritual power of a new song.
Choirs:	Through our singing we reach for new understandings of the meaning of our faith.
Leader:	Isaiah writes of melodies which spring from the hope of a new life in a liberated community.
Choirs:	We share that heritage and that hope.
Leader:	Jesus shared in a hymn at the close of the Last Supper.
Choirs:	We follow in those footsteps with awe and reverence.
Leader and Congregation:	We thank you for responding to the needs of your church by sharing your talent with us as together we worship the God of all beauty.
Choirs:	We gladly accept leadership roles in worship.

Leader and
Congregation: We pledge you our support in spirit and in fact that you may have human and material resources to undergird you.

All: Let us together worship the Lord in the beauty of holiness.[14]

Movement in Worship. . . . The relationship of movement and dance to worship is as old as the Bible itself.

CHAPTER 8

Movement in Worship

The worship of which we speak is in the active mode. This chapter is not about something that someone does to or for a congregation; rather, it is about the worship service as a medium of movement.

In *The Spirit Moves*, Carla de Sola begins the chapter on "Reflections on Dance and Prayer" with this prayer for a congregation:

> I pray that everyone, sitting cramped inside a pew, body lifeless, spine sagging and suffering, weary with weight and deadness, will be given space in which to breathe and move, will be wooed to worship with beauty and stillness, song and dance—dance charged with life, dance that lifts up both body and spirit, and we will be a holy, dancing, loving, praying and praising people.[1]

The relation of movement and dance to worship is as old as the Bible itself. Acts of the creator God are dramatic acts. "The Spirit of God was moving over the face of the waters," says Genesis 1:1. It takes the poetry of Genesis, of Isaiah, and of the psalms to convey God's creativity. God's people are on the move, whether toward the promised land, in exile, toward the temple, or as a pilgrim people. David dances before the ark of the Lord, and the psalmist urges the praise of God with dancing.

Jesus was peripatetic. He moved from place to place and taught and prayed on the way. What made his movements dramatic was that he used the elements of nature and the common life as object lessons through which the meaning of God could become clear. The Palm Sunday procession was strong pageantry as the pilgrim leader, Jesus, moved to confront the powers that be. The faith journey from Gethsemane to Golgotha is a pilgrimage that Jesus' followers make year by year as the hosannas of Palm Sunday reach Easter through the tortuous path of Maundy Thursday and Good Friday.

We are called to love God with all our heart, soul, strength, and mind. Paul puts it this way in Romans 12:1, "With eyes wide open to the mercies of God, I beg you . . . as an act of intelligent worship, to give [God] . . . your bodies, as a living sacrifice [PHILLIPS]." Thus, our worship is not just cerebral, nor should it always be witnessed from the spectator's position. Remember, we are actors in the theatre of the spirit. The whole premise of this book is that our actions must speak as loudly as our words, and that words are only one dimension of the whole pattern of our worship. Does our congregation's body language convey who we are? Does our body language convey what we're doing in a given moment of worship? If we're rejoicing, a stance of sitting or listening doesn't express those intentions. If we are offering ourselves, some form of reaching out and movement is essential.

We are strangely and wonderfully made. Through movement we can explore the meaning of space, time, and form. The patterns we make portray the range of moods of the human spirit—hope, pathos, penitence, solidarity, outreach, and caring. The lines and contours of our bodies suggest the infinite variety of the Creator's forms. Through movement we learn in fresh ways the significance of the incarnation as we experience religious truth in concrete space, time, form, and relationship.

The worship service itself is a movement experience that starts in a particular place and moves into patterns representing adoration, wonder, penitence, forgiveness, call to service, personal dedication, and celebration. These moods and meanings are part of the result of movement. To complete the process, we make a moving response to the worship service. The movements of the worship service are our way of making a conscious choice to express our intentions and feelings. Not to decide is to decide. If you make no decision about moving, you have made a negative movement choice. Rather than not move by default, it is important to make positive choices about when it is appropriate to move and when it is not.

In analyzing the place of movement in worship, one should begin with what is. Consider: What are the natural, present patterns of movement—standing, sitting, moving, or kneeling? How are heads, hands, arms, knees, and bodies engaged in worship? What kind of movement does the space itself encourage—uplifting of heads or bowing of bodies; choral processional and recessional; movement of the congregation to place offerings in the altar plate; gathering around the table for communion; or styles of greeting?

Traditional movements are standing for the call to worship, the hymns, and the scripture reading; kneeling or bowing down for prayer; sitting for the sermon; and reaching out for the kiss of peace, a fellowship circle, or greeting, as the service ends. How do these relate to the space at hand and to present practice in your congregation?

Other natural forms of movement could be instituted gradually. For example, hand gestures in relation to an anthem could be introduced, with the choir taking the modeling initiative. Also, the choir could try singing from different places in the sanctuary. Various motions could be initiated for occasional use during prayer, such as kneeling or bowing low for confession, holding palms open for the pastoral and intercessory prayers, and joining hands with neighbors for prayers of thanksgiving or benedictions.

We have tried to suggest that movement in worship is inevitable. It is essential to consider the way movement is used and to be intentional about its use. The pastor or the worship leader can encourage intentional movement in a service in a variety of ways. This chapter suggests some ideas that have been used in a variety of settings. These ideas are intended to stimulate your imagination so you can create your own appropriate forms of movement.

The role and initiative of the pastor or the worship leader are central to the way movement is used or new patterns are introduced. The basic elements of the worship service are carried out by her or him. Such leadership needs to be confident and well prepared, for to act hesitatingly or in an unclear manner is to foster chaos and jeopardize the new opportunity. Because worship matters so much to so many, doing a bad job or introducing change in an inept manner creates a negative impression that may seem out of proportion to the character of the change.

Sometimes the leadership role involves sanctioning or blessing particular ventures—the role of the choir, patterns of prayer, or participation of instrumentalists or a sacred dance group. More often, leadership directs or participates in the movements, and the congregation follows that lead.

One exciting paradigm comes to us from many centuries of experience. The windows in the cathedral in Chartres, France are among the most magnificent in the world. Their color, Chartres blue, has a special place in the history of sacred design. The windows tell the story of the Bible, the gospel, and Christian history. What was more natural than to make them the focal points for worship and education? Until recent years there were no pews in the cathedral, so the congregation could easily move from window to window. This created a powerful sense of motion, enhanced by light, color, and symbol. Each stop became an occasion for adoration, prayer, storytelling, commissioning, and consecration. The liturgy, the work of the people, was literally a pilgrimage, as people moved from window to window to savor and celebrate the Christian story.

Although most present-day churches have stationary pews and may lack the majesty of the Chartres windows, they do have symbolic elements—windows, symbols, spaces and places, art forms, and colors—that contain their own story and convey their special Christian significance. Sometimes, like the priests of Chartres, the congregation can move from place to place as they focus upon this symbol, or that art form, or patterns of color, light, and space. If the congregation is large, several people can be trained to share the leadership of smaller groups. Try a series of lenten sermons centered on different facets of the sanctuary and its resources, with appropriate movements to illuminate the story. Ideally, the congregation should position itself to take advantage of the day's focus. Slides or dance or choral music can augment the worship leader's role and the movement of the congregation in relation to its space.

The Rhythm of Worship: Adoration

Let's explore more concrete possibilities as they relate to the four elements of worship examined in chapter 2, namely, adoration, confession, acceptance, and response. What is essential at the outset of the worship experience is the transition of the gathered community from its scattered world to focusing on the stage of the spirit. This is a physical pilgrimage that is often a harried one, marked by ambivalence or conflict or hostility.

No dramatist just lets the play begin. Careful attention to the opening is vital. In *Dancin'* Bob Fosse literally takes the audience through the process of setting the lights at the proper angle and color. Other dramatists start off with an empty stage, as darkening houselights draw the audience to the coming action. For another playwright the darkened stage gradually reveals human form that is soon to spring into action. Sometimes, as the curtain opens, we seem to have stumbled into the midst of an ongoing scene, and our minds do a double take as we get with the action. The worship planners must somehow convey to the rest of us actors in the theatre of the spirit that we are onstage and that the play is beginning.

If a dramatic processional of the whole congregation is possible, this can give body to the notion of moving into holy space, expressing adoration with the whole person. If the whole congregation does not process, worship leaders and choir can do so as the congre-

The Rhythm of Worship. . . . Often leadership will direct or participate in the movements, and the congregation will follow the lead; therefore it is important to be confident and well prepared.

gation's standing posture celebrates the moods of adoration and expectation. In some Eastern religion worship rites, the worshipers clap their hands to get God's attention. It's as if they were saying, "Listen up, God!"

One church often places a call-to-worship type phrase to be said out loud in the bulletins of the first few arrivals. Sometimes the phrase is scriptural, sometimes it describes what the worshiper brings or seeks, and sometimes it defines the world into which the gospel is borne that day. Always the sentence is numbered, so that the call to worship begins with various persons arising spontaneously, by number, from the congregation to share their written call to worship. If you try this in your church, be sure the first person knows when to begin.

Another church asks people to brush off their bodies whatever they have come in with, such as the dust of the road, the burdens of the week, their angers and irritations, their ambivalence about being there, their sense of estrangement from other people and from this environment, their sense of distance from God and their best selves. Then, people are asked to use arm movements to take on a new self, a new intentionality. Philippians 2:5-7 is the scriptural warrant for this process. Paul asks us to have the same mind as Jesus, who "emptied himself" and took on a new form—that of servant. We brush off the past and our impediments so we can put on a new garment of openness and expectation.

Another variation is to take advantage of a warm day, when people are overdressed. Encourage worshipers to remove their jackets. This can be an occasion for symbolic openness of the self to the breath of the spirit. It should be accompanied by a simulated putting on of the garments of new intention and promise. These motions of taking off and putting on can be done before people enter the sanctuary, or they can be done as part of the adoration or confession phase of the worship service.

Conditioned as we are to thinking of worship as a spectator sport, none of this will be easy or natural. Its aim is to help us love God with all our being, to worship God in the beauty of holiness and in our wholeness. People can be helped to get in touch with the elements of worship as their bodies can express these. We stand for the processional and the singing of a hymn. We smile in response to the preacher's "Good morning" or in reflecting the exuberant joy of an adoration hymn. As we sing, we should look up in a mood of outreach and exaltation. The sense of awe and wonder can be shown by reaching arms and fingertips as high as they will go and by standing on tiptoe. Swaying our bodies from side to side in response to the music and rhythm helps convey the mood. These movements should be horizontal as well as vertical (if there is enough room) so that one can be in touch with one's body and the space it occupies.

Another approach uses pictures cut from magazines and mounted on cardboard (old shirt cardboard or cut-up file folders will do nicely) or construction paper. The pictures should show the everyday events and experiences of people. Some might illustrate a naturally religious situation, but they should not appear to be staged or have an aura of fixed piety about them. A theme is chosen—your doubts, hopes, dreams, convictions, celebrations. Each person is asked to choose a picture that expresses her or his image of this theme. Persons then share their pictures and their meanings in conversation with others near them.

One variation of this is to illustrate, in movement, an important idea or conviction, like, What are my hopes for today's service? or, What is my understanding of faith? or, For what am I thankful today? Such movement can be done individually or shared in groups of two or three in the pew. Or encourage a group of two to four persons to choose a single picture and then to develop a group statue depicting action, faith, or meaning as expressed in the picture. By using pictures and movement we hope to stimulate imaginations and enhance the sense of corporateness in worship. Together let us adore the holy One.

Still another way to introduce movement into the adoration phase of the service is for the worship leader to use a call to worship or a litany of adoration and praise that includes responses from the congregation. With music, scripture, or poetic reading, the leader does appropriate movements, to be repeated by the congregation. "Outwitted," by Edwin Markham, is an excellent choice for this purpose.

> He drew a circle that shut me out—
> Heretic, rebel, a thing to flout,
> But love and I had the wit to win:
> We drew a circle that took him in.[2]

Dancers do a movement to each phrase as it is read. Or the leader does a movement pattern, followed by the whole congregation repeating the pattern.

Or Psalm 150 could be read, with the organ responding in the various instrument voices on the keyboard—trumpet, flute, strings.

Sometimes a *bidding prayer* is used in a service. The leader invites, or bids, persons to pray for a special subject or person, and after each bidding the congregation makes a response. This response could be made using movement: prayer for the presence of the Spirit with hands receptively open, confession with arms folded and heads bowed, reconciliation with neighbor through outstretched arms and hands, the search for peace with hands linked in a global circle. Rich images are impressive, diverse, and almost unlimited. For example, Anne Squire, in an article on spirituality, tells of the delight of her congregation when, in her prayer, she thanked God for the smell of chili sauce, the taste of crabapple jelly, and the sight of a freezer overflowing with vegetables.[3] Let your imagination run as you seek ways to express adoration, awe, and wonder.

Confession

Our bodily postures convey our intentions and our moods. This is perhaps more fully realized in the confession/penitence phase than in any other mood of worship. Sitting relaxed with hands turned palm upward is a posture of openness and readiness to receive the Spirit. Folding arms across one's body symbolizes the holding in, the withdrawal of oneself from God and from others. Kneeling or bowing the head and body communicate penitence and contriteness. The uplifting of eyes, head, arms, and spirit expresses the receiving of forgiveness and the reaching out for new energy and possibilities.

Confession has to do with alienation from God and neighbor. Ask each person, during confession time, to think about someone in the congregation with whom he or she has unfinished business; to pray for forgiveness, for insight into how to approach this person, for courage to develop an empathetic stance; and then to approach this person after the service. "So if you are offering your gift at the altar, and there remember that your [sister or] brother has something against you, leave your gift there . . . and go; first be reconciled . . . and then come and offer your gift [Matt. 5:23-24]."

In addition to the natural body movements that accompany the element of confession in worship, there are a variety of ways to enact its meaning. One way is to ask people to imagine boxes in which they carry things they want to shed. Ask them to pretend that they have these boxes in their hands, to shape them and hold them firmly. Let your imagination run. What things are in the boxes? How did they get there? Why do we have them, anyway? How attached are we to them? How free are we to let them go?

There are a couple of ways to empty the boxes. Using pantomime, the boxes can be passed from one person to another, until they are all at the center of the aisle. Then they may be offered up as part of a confessional act. A sentence spoken by the worship leader can celebrate the gathering of the boxes. Or simulate the running of cleansing water through the box to remove the impediments. Again, the worship leader's sentence confirms this cleansing process.

Another participatory confession pattern involves pieces of paper inserted in the bulletins or placed in the pews. On them persons are asked to write something they want to eliminate from their lives. These papers can be placed in the offering plate or burned in a container that is safe. Each person should place his or her own paper in the container. The worship leader can offer a prayer receiving these offerings and celebrating the new beginnings they represent.

If there is an active group of sacred dancers in the church, they might do dance patterns to elements of confession, as in Psalm 42. The dance could be done in silence as the congregation reads the text, or it may be done to music or performed in time with the spoken word.

Acceptance

The acceptance element is two-dimensional—God's acceptance of us and our acceptance of God. A variety of movement patterns can express this. A statement of faith can be said or sung together or responsively, or a responsive reading can alternate voices or sections from the congregation.

Through movement the worship leader or a sacred dance group can show the interplay of God's acceptance and our own. Symbolic patterns include clasped hands, the circle, and the embrace. The congregation can participate in these patterns, following the initiative of the worship leader, the choir, or the dance group.

We have mentioned standing as an appropriate posture in which to receive the scripture, especially the reading from the Gospels. The word Selah often appears with the psalms (Psalm 3 is illustrative). This Hebrew word means literally "Imagine that!"—words of adoration, delight, and affirmation. Encourage the congregation to use "Selah" at appropriate moments, in response to the scripture reading.

At specified points during the sermon, the congregation can make standing, sitting, or kneeling responses. The experience of the black church in using amens and oral responses to prayer and sermon is suggestive.

Earlier we told of the church that used characters from *The Wiz* to help its lenten sermon series and worship events take on a dramatic quality. Creative use of contemporary dramatic material can enhance our worship.

From time to time a values clarification device may be used in connection with the sermon. There are five postures through which we express our response: a thumb waved vigorously, high in the air, indicates strong agreement; the stationary, uplifted thumb signifies agreement; folded arms connote neutrality; a thumbs-down pattern means disagreement; and strong waving of the down-turned thumb signals intense dissent. In a sermon on the Holy Spirit, for example, the preacher can test the waters with such statements as these:

The notion of the Holy Spirit has no meaning for me.

The Holy Spirit is another name for God.

It helps me to think of the Spirit as She.

I feel I am actively in touch with God's Spirit.

Our thumbs or arms will go to work to convey our response to such questions. The worship leader and the congregation have real data to work with, and the congregation has a new, publicly declared stake in the sermon. One ground rule is that people have a right not to vote on any given question.

University Church (Disciples of Christ and United Church of Christ) in Chicago uses an interesting pattern to receive new members. Persons being received are asked to say something about themselves and their interest in the church. After formal words of celebration, affirmation, and prayer, the congregation stands and says to each new member in turn, "We welcome you, ———, and we name you as one of us." After each person is named, the congregation repeats these words together: "We vow to share our life and faith with you. Please share your life and faith with us."

Response

Whether through placing our offering on the plate at the altar, extending the hand of fellowship, giving the kiss of peace to our neighbor, or moving into a specific action project, the response segment, by definition, demands an active component.

The importance of an active offering response has already been established. Presenting pledges for the church budget can be another occasion for persons to physically move forward to the chancel and lay their gifts or pledges on the altar.

A hymn of dedication and commitment helps us to begin our

response to the grace of the worship service. A vocal benediction or a sung response to the benediction, such as "God Be with You 'Til We Meet Again," are other appropriate vehicles to show our response to the holy.

A fellowship circle, the joining of hands in the pews, or an embrace can express our solidarity in common response to the challenge of the holy God.

An important individual response pattern may be suggested by the worship leader and/or the bulletin: Each person during the response segment of the service is asked to pick out another person for whom they plan to do some loving act. The bulletin can say something like, "Rough out in your own mind what you wish to do and how to do it; then, when the worship service has ended, do it!"

Theme Interpretation Through Movement

Worship in a fellowship or church school setting is usually built upon a theme. This setting and the use of a theme may give the worship planner more of an opportunity to incorporate movement patterns than the Sunday morning sanctuary setting.

Community is an example of a theme for such a setting. Participants move single file into the worship space. The spiritual "Jesus Walked This Lonesome Valley" is an appropriate processional. The room is set with a circle of chairs (or two circles, if size requires it). After a call to worship (perhaps the one on page 13) and prayer, the leader indicates that this day the meaning of community is to be pursued. This relates to our own sense of self and solitariness and to our relationships with other persons. We begin with ourselves and then move on to others.

First, persons are asked to get in touch with their own body and the space it occupies. Each person should find a spot on the floor, some distance away from anyone else, where he or she can explore arms, legs, torso, and bodily positions. Worshipers are asked to feel, touch, and enjoy the sensation of head, chest, arms, legs, and to turn their heads from place to place, to get a sense of vista and vision. Lying down gives one a different perspective on space and one's relationship to it. The leader offers directions like "Push the small of your back," or, "Kick your legs in the air," or, "Stand up and jump in place."

Then it is time to move together, toward one another, and to greet one another using only their elbows. It is possible to do the same pattern of greeting using the forehead, back, shoulders, hands, and arms. After the greetings the group joins hands and engages in simple movement toward one another. An appropriate scripture may be read, such as I Corinthians 12:12-27 for the inward-facing circle; and then, as the group drops and rejoins hands, facing outward, Luke 4:14-19.

From their places in the circle—or back in the chair circle, if you prefer—two or three people share their thoughts about the meaning of community and of solidarity. The group then moves out of the worship area, using a hymn like "Blest Be the Tie That Binds" or "God of Grace and God of Glory" or "They'll Know We Are Christians by Our Love."

Another exciting theme you could develop is that of *praise*, with dancing as the medium. Psalm 150:4 counsels us to praise God with "tambourines and dancing." A key insight is from Corita, who said, "If we left it to the spirit, all we would have is Jesus and dancing." The key music could be Sydney Carter's hymn, "Lord of the Dance."

We once watched a group that sought to express symbols for God using finger paints as the medium. Each person was asked to interpret and defend the gobs of paint on butcher paper, which represented his or her particular expression of the deity. The examples given in this section are offered as stimuli, to rouse your imagination to do movement that is right for you and for your people, space, and setting.

Dancers and Dance Groups

There is a difference between group-involving exercises, participatory dance, and performed dance. Our comments in this chapter, until now, have suggested simple patterns of movement in worship by which all of us can express our intentions with our whole bodies. This section deals specifically with dancers and dance groups. It assumes that a choreographer-director will be chosen. Perhaps a dance workshop and auditions will take place. In any case, a serious dance group will be formed under competent leadership.

Isadora Duncan said that "unless dance is religious, it is mere merchandise."[4] Dance is a whole body enterprise that touches and engages mind, spirit, and gut. Full of dreary routine, good dance also reaches the intuitive and deeply felt yearnings of the dancer. The great meanings of life we call religious are caught up in dance: pain, pleasure, ecstasy, faith, fidelity, forgiveness, aspiration, depression, hope, love, and grace.

If a church intends to form a dance group, the church leadership

Dancers and Dance Groups. . . . Through dance and drama we learn in fresh ways the meaning of the incarnation. Clockwise: dancing sermon, Cathedral of St. John the Divine, New York City; symbolic cross, Christ United Methodist Church, New York City; *Godspell,* Cathedral of St. John the Divine, New York City; rhythmic choir, Highlands Church, Melrose, MA.

needs to be supportive and encouraging. Doing serious dance with a voluntary organization is difficult in any case, but if the church's leadership is negative or apathetic, it is uphill all the way. Dancing well requires talent and infinite practice. There are no shortcuts.

The leadership of a dance group itself needs to be confident and well prepared. A choreographer should be clear about what he or she is doing. Part of this is understanding the church in which the group will function: its convictions, style, expectations, and commitments. Another part is in understanding the space being used for performance. Get a sense of its promise and limitations and the ways it can enhance or inhibit the possibilities of dance. Think of how light, color, and form are able to give shape to that space and make it more attractive.

If you are not sure where to begin, review the material on community on page 133. That suggests a way whereby bodies may begin to get in touch with one another. Before dance rehearsals begin, the leader should have worked her or his way through the various movements in front of a mirror or with a partner, so as not to waste the group's time. Careful preparation helps build the confidence that is essential for effective performance.

It is important to know the medium and some of its possibilities. Films and videotapes are available and may be rented or borrowed from a library, a dance or television studio, or a media buff. A variety of good dance books is available in most large bookstores located in urban areas.

Where one starts with a dance group depends upon how much dance experience the members of the group have had. But no matter how little or how much experience they have had, they will still have to be welded into an ensemble, so that they can develop their own style and response to the choreographer. Warm-up basics are essential for any group—beginning or experienced. Only repetition and insistent practice can prevent an inhibited or embarrassed performance.

Variety is the spice of dance as it is of life. Dance need not always be "pretty." Often it is strong, even grotesque. It can reflect the depths as well as the heights of human experience. No one choreographer can express all the possibilities inherent in a group or a theme. It is, therefore, important to draw upon various choreographers for fresh insight.

In working with a new group, a good place to begin is to simulate and experience the growth of a flower, from the closed-up bulb through the various growth processes until the full flowering is completed. This can be done to music. A good piece is "Chinon" from *Lion in Winter*. At the outset each person "grows" in response to her or his perception of musical patterns. Later such movements can be put together into a precise choreographic routine. Be a perennial: end the cycle of a season and begin again!

Dancers should be helped to develop basic body patterns related to the various moods or elements in worship. The sense of mood needs to be active and visceral. Dancers should move from place to place in purposeful but developing patterns. The sense of humbleness before the holy can be conveyed in a prostrate position or in kneeling or with one's head deeply bowed. The outreach or upreach from the humbled position can reflect a sense of forgiveness, the reaching out for new life, and the search for new promise. The joining of hands and their reach upward embody the circle of acceptance and the solidarity of a support community.

Help the group experience such moods as anger, alienation, penitence, and exaltation. Through movement the dance group can express these moods in the Adam and Eve story, the good Samaritan narrative, the Lord's Prayer, and the Beatitudes. This material can be read in the background or patterned out in the choreography. Tunes from musicals like *Godspell, Jesus Christ Superstar,* and *Joseph and the Amazing Technicolor Dreamcoat* offer other ideas for dance patterns.

Simple props can help enormously in fostering and sharing imagination. Masks can be powerfully effective. Flags and streamers on sticks enhance a group's performance. Use your imagination, and don't neglect what's close at hand.

A major role of the director or choreographer of the group is to assist dancers in doing what they can do best. As one gets to know the dancers, they will reveal their strengths and weaknesses. It is important, of course, both to teach patterns and to help dancers feel their way into them, so that they can convey to others the meaning of a piece or movement from the inside, from the depths of their own being. Just as important, view these performers from the perspective of the audience or congregation. How does the group look? Are movements and patterns clear? What do they communicate?

The Guest Dance Group

Inviting a dance group to perform can be an important occasion for any church. Someone should be designated to provide invitations and to make arrangements and linkage. Everyone involved should know who is responsible for what. What is expected—the when, where, who, how, and why—should be clearly interpreted to the dancers or to their leader, and those understandings negotiated with all concerned, so that choreographer and church leaders are all on the same wavelength. For all concerned, it is a good idea to put these understandings in writing.

The visiting dancers should have an opportunity to practice in the intended space and under as near performance conditions as possible. Those who will be helping with the performance—light and sound people, musicians, worship leaders—should be on hand to rehearse, as desired by the choreographer.

The coming of the dance group should be anticipated. Those who prepare newspaper articles and the church newsletter and bulletin should be clear about the group's name and its history, style, and repertoire and should interpret the occasion to the church and to the larger public. Will it be a concert, or a worship service? What arrangements will prevail: ticket sales, offering, entrance of congregation and dancers, occasion for conversation with the performers, interpretive material in the bulletin or program?

Give careful consideration to how the dancers will be accommodated in the church building. Will there be a dressing room or similar space? Clothes, purses, and personal belongings need to be put somewhere that is safe. What about towels (dancing is a sweaty business)? accessible bathrooms? water? place for props? space for warm-ups? piano? snacks?

If this is the church's first venture with an outside dance group, the planners should anticipate the event carefully. Talk to some members of the congregation in advance to discover what is in their heads about this event, and help them understand the why and the how. Take advantage of the grapevine. Try to see the dancers and their performance through the new eyes of the anticipating congregation.

Two integrities are involved: the church's and the dancers'. Both must be taken into account as the invitation is extended and plans for the performance are concluded, so that expectations for the event don't differ. Such expectations should be made as clear as possible at the outset. The church may ask the dancers to do something that, in their integrity, is impossible, or the dancers may seek to perform material that the church considers offensive. Hopefully, the dancers and the church will grow through the experience, with the church's understanding of worship being enlarged and the dancer's experiencing the acceptance of their gifts as an act of grace.

Although these comments pertain to a guest dance group, we recommend that the same procedures and criteria be used for any visiting performing group, whether dramatic, musical, or dance.

It is important to understand empathetically a dancer's world and world view. Rey reflected on what it's like to be a dancer:

I am a dancer. I cannot remember when first I knew that, but it came to me as naturally as breathing or sleeping. Long before the endless hours of routine, the searing reflections of the practice mirror, and the struggle to make my limbs behave, I knew that the rhythmic yearnings of my body were not to be denied.

I am my body. When I dance, I know myself to be whole. I feel vibrantly alive. My heart pounds. My blood marches. My muscles hop to attention. My skin becomes wet with its own dew. My pores steam out an aura of heat. I have discovered my body is as stretchable as warm taffy; and as brittle as a dry twig. All the parts of my body support a single intention. My arms, legs, muscles, shoulders, head, torso, and brain all work together like a well-oiled, finely-tuned machine. My body reaches new vistas like an explorer in unmapped lands. As a dancer, I am a mass of contradictions—battered shins, bunions, and bruises; yet, arms and arches as graceful as a butterfly floating through the gentle summer. I am stiff. I am free. As I toss my head, my hair whips briskly through the air. It is cool and clammy as it clings to my face. I am my body with all its endearing possibilities and its menacing limitations, its sensual pleasure, and its unending pain.

I am my space. A piece of the stage is mine. The contours of my journey are mapped. I am part of all I touch—the solidness of the wooden floor supports me, the surrounding air invites me, the flickering light and shadow chase me. My feet leave the ground as a soaring bird. I dart now here, now there. The sinews of my body stretch their bounds, yet I am rooted in gravity's space.

I am my rhythms. I learned to swim in the changing tides of music. I respond to its momentary silences and its multitude of sounds. I pulse to its vibrations. In the deep core of my being I house my own drummer. The music and rhythm of my dancing flows from my drummer's depths. Motion and melody are mated like star-crossed lovers.

I am my community. My moves, sounds, breathings, and extensions mirror others. Together, we make a kaleidoscope—arm with arm, leg with leg, and head with head. My being is assaulted with flying droplets of sweat. They are salty, warm, and heady. The staccato pops of noisy joints are like a crackling fire. Eroticism is present in the scent, sight, and touch of our swirling bodies. We flow like the ocean's waves, pounding, insistent, and awesome.

I am a dancer. In that identity, my body and my being are one. The rhythms of my body, enhanced by music, give birth to new reaches of the spirit, to unknown possibilities of form. I share in a community of person, movement, and space. Together we paint a living picture. I am a dancer, now and always.[5]

Educational Development and Worship. . . . A biblical story can be retold in contemporary terms or with a modern parable that will make the story come alive.

CHAPTER 9

Educational Development and Worship

We humans have a sense of the passing of seasons even in climates where nature's changes seem undramatic. The moods of our spirit relate to those changes and to the stages of our own growth; therefore, our worship is interwoven with the seasons of the spirit. After extensive studies of people's experience, Daniel J. Levinson has written a whole book about life's seasons. "To speak of seasons," he contends,

> is to say that the life course has a certain shape, that it evolves through a series of definable forms. A season is a relatively stable segment of the total cycle. Summer has a character different from that of winter; twilight is different from sunrise. To say that a season is relatively stable, however, does not mean that it is stationary or static. Change goes on within each, and a transition is required for the shift from one season to the next. Every season has its own time; it is important in its own right and needs to be understood in its own terms. No season is better or more important than any other. Each has its necessary place and contributes its special character to the whole. It is an organic part of the total cycle, linking past and future and containing both within itself.[1]

Sacramental forms correspond to key elements in human development. Baptism happens at the beginning of life and celebrates God's grace as well as the sustenance of the caring fellowship of Christians. Confirmation takes notice of the adult faith decision and full passage into the believing community. To celebrate communion is to re-claim community and to renew faith. Marriage celebrates a covenant between two people. Rituals of bereavement mark the impact of the deceased and anticipate the resurrection.

Developmental Stages

A number of people have given attention to the stages of human development. Jean Piaget's work on the developing life of children is the foundation for much of this understanding.[2] He contends that the first two years are primarily *sensory*. Years two through six are seen as *intuitive* or prelogical. Ages seven through eleven Piaget describes as *concrete* operations, quite specific, and mechanical moves. Beyond the age of twelve, persons reach the stage of *formal* operations, where their own understanding and imagination help them form patterns of meaning and movement. They become self-determining individuals.

Lawrence Kohlberg has built upon Piaget's work, and he identifies stages of *moral development*. James Fowler has made an analysis of *faith development* stages. Erik Erikson, operating within the premises of Freudian psychology, has documented eight stages of *psychosocial development*. Gwen Kennedy Neville and John Westerhoff III have applied some of these understandings to *liturgy and education*. Earlier in this chapter we referred to the work done by Daniel Levinson on adult seasons. Many of these understandings have been popularized by Gail Sheehy in her book *Passages*.[3] We draw upon the work of these researchers and authors as they touch the theatre of the spirit.

Each age has its business to do. The *youngest child's* world represents the struggle for care, nurture, food, dryness, and warmth. The world changes as the child moves from lying to crawling to standing to walking, and from primordial noises to symbolic sound. As Piaget observed, it is a sensory world. Erikson defines the essential task of the age as dealing with trust versus mistrust. For the youngest child the physical world and the spiritual world are closely interwoven and are mediated through parents and close ones. Religious concepts such as trust, forgiveness, love, and grace are experienced more than verbalized.

James Fowler calls the first faith-stage the *intuitive-projective* and sees it happening during ages *four through seven*. Of the child at stage one he says that

> there is little ability as yet to take the role of others. The child is not yet able to construct and interpret the inner feelings, intentions or reasoning of other persons. Interaction with others therefore is largely a matter of moment to moment parallel behavior, as in playing.[4]

Language about faith is borrowed from others. The stage is more active than verbal but is capable of some imagination. Bruno

Bettelheim indicates that fairy tales may provide important connections with children's experience because they touch children's imaginations and because they aid in the good/evil sorting-out process.[5]

Thus, in the first few years of life, play and worship are closely intertwined. This may be, after all, how God intended it to be for all of us, for Jesus, you remember, said that we cannot enter the kingdom except we become like children. For young children worship needs to be intentional and distinctive but closely linked with the important people in their lives and with their moment-to-moment experiencing.

Fowler calls the second stage *mythic-literal faith*. He describes the six- to eleven-year-old in this way:

> Concrete operational thinking has developed. Fluidity of concepts and symbolism has diminished. The child is concerned to understand lawfulness and predictability in relations between persons and in conditions affecting one's life. There is a strong empirical bent fostering an experimental approach as regards the tangible world.
>
> Symbols for deity, where used, are typically anthropomorphic. They have power to cause and make; but they also have feelings and will and are attentive to the intentions of humans.
>
> Narrative ability is now well developed. There is interest in myths and heroic images. One-dimensionality and literalism mark efforts to "explain" that which myth and symbols try to convey.[6]

For Erikson, the age is one that reflects the conflict between industry and inferiority. The child is trying to develop the capacity to do, to cope, and to create, at the same time living on the edge of failure and of self-doubt. Erikson assumes that the industry stage will build upon the achievements of trust, autonomy, and initiative achieved in earlier stages.

Worship that is expressive of the world of the elementary-age child uses myth and symbol creatively. The notions of the exodus of the Hebrews from Egypt, the personality of Jesus, the loyalty of Mary Magdalene, and the adventures of Paul are motifs that appeal. Parents and teachers need to make connections with movies, television, and cultural patterns that reach faith's meanings; *Star Wars* and *Superman*, for instance, are religiously suggestive in their experience.

A great deal is made these days of the concept of story—each of us has a special faith story. The Bible is seen as a book of faith stories. Jesus, of course, used such a concept in his parables. A biblical story can be retold either in contemporary terms or with a modern parable that makes the story come alive. Use your imagination, and help the children use theirs. "All the world is a stage," and on it we act out our stories. Drama is highly participative; it reveals what is in people's depths in ways other media cannot.

The movement into adolescence is a crucial time. John Westerhoff describes the religious experience of early childhood as "experienced faith" and that of the elementary years as "affiliative faith."[7] His term for the adolescent years is "searching faith," and he suggests a covenant of discipleship, to be made by young people on the thirteenth anniversary of their baptism.

Fowler describes the faith of the teen years as *synthetic-conventional*.

> The person, now able to see himself/herself *as being seen by a variety of significant others* who occupy a variety of disparate standpoints in his/her world, has the problem of synthesizing those mirror images. Moreover, congruence must be found between his/her feelings and images of self and the world and those held by others.[8]

Life is strongly group-oriented, and the issue of identity is central to one whose body and world are changing. It is a time of sorting and evaluating, an occasion for determining appropriate role models and life authorities.

In worship the use of story can be augmented by biography and autobiography. The adolescent wonders if anyone ever "felt this way" or "traveled this road" before. Biography can provide the mirror of reflection, imagination, and understanding. If the men and women of the Bible and the Christian tradition are to come alive for this generation, it will happen through a process of identification. The generation gap is a chasm of communication, symbols, and feelings, not of age and life-experience. The adolescent perceives the world through all the senses; thus, various artistic media and sensory forms are essential to celebrate passages and pilgrimages.

The late adolescent/early adult stage often has what Fowler calls *individuating-reflexive faith*. Faith is more internal and selective. To a larger extent, I become by own authority for my faith and morals. Experimentation continues, and trying on for size is characteristic. Erikson speaks of it as the *intimacy* versus *isolation* stage. Levinson describes the task of early young adulthood as fashioning a "provisional structure that provides a workable link between the valued self and the adult society."[9]

Fowler describes the faith components of the young adult stage:

The ability to reflect critically on one's faith has appeared. There is awareness that one's outlook is vulnerable and can shift, and also of the relativity of one's way of experiencing to that of others whose outlook and loyalties are different.

There is an awareness of one's world view as an explicit system. There is a concern for inner consistency, integration and comprehensiveness. Stage 4 typically has an ideological quality. There is an excess of assimilation over accommodation, of subjective over objective content. Differences with other world views are sharply recognized. . . .

The hope and need is for affiliation with a group and its ideology which provides a style of living and seeing which both express and hold up models for further development of one's own individuating faith.[10]

Relevant worship expresses the transitional nature of early young adulthood. At the same time, worship should reflect the search for and the finding of community so important to persons in this stage. Role models and faith symbols are significant at this time of life. Meaning clues can be found by using contemporary music and the "top forty" charts as themes for worship and some liturgical forms. Attention should be given to the desire to find sustaining community and to build strong ideological consistency. Many of the most attractive biblical people were themselves young adults facing the challenges of vocation, sexual identity, belief structure, and community; examples are Jesus, Mary, Jeremiah, Paul, Timothy, Deborah, Moses, Miriam, David, and Esther.

Fowler calls his stage five *paradoxical-consolidative* faith. In this stage considerable personal autonomy exists. Experience and understanding are consolidated so that a consistent pattern of faith is developed. The paradox is that while one's faith is clear and compelling, one is especially aware of the faith of others, which may differ or even be contradictory. "Stage five," says Fowler, "is ready for community of identification beyond tribal, racial, class or ideological boundaries. To be genuine, it must know the cost of such community and be prepared to pay the cost."[11]

Although this stage in middle adulthood is a time of consolidation, it is also a time of reaching out. Levinson describes this period as facing four polarities: the interplay of young and old, of the creative and the destructive, of the masculine and the feminine in each person, and the mutuality of attachment and separateness.[12] For Erikson, this is the period of *generativity* versus *stagnation*.

Carl Jung did the basic work that has led to identifying the *Midlife Transition*.[13] He distinguished two halves of life, with the fulcrum point around age forty, the period he called "the noon of life." It is a time, Jung emphasized, with a resurgence of *individuation*, the process of unique self-understanding and generative self-determination.

The faith and worship implications are clear. The settled/nomadic conflict is within us and in our midst; therefore, some elements of our life, like the symbolic, must be dependable. God helps us develop our settled interior places; God is our ground, our nurturer, and our covenant partner. But God is also a journeying, dynamic reality. Faith is not static; its symbol is not the hammock. Praying on one's knees is active. Jesus is recognized by his followers in the breaking of bread or while journeying on the road. The dramatic elements of the Christian year convey this sense of dynamic movement through the pathos and hope of human experience.

Fowler identifies a sixth stage in faith development: *universalizing*. It is a rare stage, generally associated with mature adulthood but not reached by the majority of persons at any age. It is characterized by the capacity to think and relate in broad terms that reach beyond the narrow particularities which often separate persons from one another.

There is a maturity of age and stage that is universal as persons face their later years—the stage Levinson calls late adulthood. Erikson sees it as the conflict of *integrity* versus *despair*. Substantial freedom of choice usually exists with regard to time and to activity. Levinson describes the situation in part: "[We] can devote [ourselves] in a serious-playful way to the interests that flow most directly from the depths of the self. Using the youthfulness still within [us], [we] can enjoy the creative possibilities of this season."[14]

Worship approaches that address the later years need to take full account of the ambiguity of that experience. Much of life is in the past. The mantle has, in significant part, been passed on to others. Wisdom and experience are to be honored. Intergenerational possibilities are strong as life-experiences are shared. Older persons may be uniquely aware of the meaning of freedom and the process of sorting out priorities. If the young "see visions," as Joel contends, the old "dream dreams [2:28]." Both are the stuff of faith, community, and living out of our creation in the image of God.

These faith stages are suggestive and have a bearing on worship planning for children or youth or adults. They also remind us that in every given worship setting, people will be at different places in their experience, believing, and expectations. Worship forms need to express these diverse needs as well as to nurture faith in its several modes.

Note especially how important the symbolic element is in faith experience and development. Jesus used the symbolic to anchor faith—faith is like a mustard seed; the people of faith are like salt, leaven, and light; Peter is a rock (the Greek *Petra* means "rock") and is to be the solidness "on which I will build my church."

Note, too, that the pattern in faith development is from the other-directed to the self-directed. The influences of others and of scripture and tradition continue to make their claim, but increasingly it is my faith, my credo, my trust, and my assent.

Penelope Washbourn, in *Becoming Woman*, identifies the stages of human development.

> The life of a woman is like the life of every living creature; it is a series of transitions involving death and rebirth. In human beings, emotional and spiritual development is, however, not inevitable. We do *choose;* we are free to effect what we become even at the last moment of our life. Sometimes we despair that nothing can be done; we have been determined by our childhood, our society, our culture, our age, and there is no hope.[15]

Washbourn identifies that, in each instance, these moments of choice have a graceful and a demonic component. We are free to live, and to choose to live, gracefully or demonically. There seems to be in each choice the divine and the demon. Our worship needs to present both the radical character of our choosing and the mix of good/evil, graceful/demonic that is in everything.

Learning to Worship

Every human being has a yearning to worship, but this yearning is not activated automatically. Thus, one's capacity for worship must be nurtured. "Stir into flame the gift of God that is within you," is the way Paul puts it (2 Tim. 1:6, NEB).

Chapter 1 reviewed some of the ways we learn to worship. They involve strengthening our intuitive capacities, raising our consciousness about the meaning and patterns of worship, imitating the actions of others, and sharing in the search for authentic worship. C. Ellis Nelson, in exploring "where faith begins," contends that "faith is communicated by a community of believers and . . . the meaning of faith is developed by its members out of their history, by

Learning to Worship. . . . All human beings have a yearning to worship, but worship will not happen automatically, thus our capacity for it must be nurtured.

their interaction with each other, and in relation to the events that take place in their lives."[16]

The word education means literally to "lead out." Meaning is drawn from within a person so that she or he is enabled to move from a known place to new space; however, education is not just "done to" another, for we bring our own experiences to the learning situation and these experiences become the context in which we appropriate the new. Thus, there is a mutuality in the learning process. This is particularly true of learning *about* and learning *to* worship.

A congregation has a style of life, or a personality, in which people are socialized. We might call this the congregation's body language. That language includes a sense of history, excitement about projects, patterns of prayer and devotion, recognition of the power of certain symbols and symbolic acts, valuing the arts, and patterns of leadership and sharing. It may also reflect the racist, sexist, or parochial character of the congregation.

James M. Gustafson speaks of the way in which a church becomes a moral community.[17] People must be intentional about this for it to happen. Key elements are standing in a given moral tradition, talking about it, and doing something to express ethical conviction. A moral tradition has certain phrases and words to express its nuances. The church is, in Gustafson's phrase, "a community of moral discourse."

Every congregation stands in some cultural tradition that has distinguishing characteristics. Part of "roots education" involves the contemporary celebration of these unique heritages, like the Welsh hymn tunes, the German chorales, the spirituals from the Black experience, or Our Lady of Guadalupe from the Hispanic tradition. The recovery of these elements need exclude no one; in fact, they can be offered and celebrated as gifts from a rich past.

Both worship and education are social acts. They have to do with our being and our belonging, as well as with specific actions. When Margaret Mead was asked what a child needs in order to avoid being stunted in development, she answered:

> First, a child needs food and water and rest. But these are not enough. A child also needs the warmth and security of at least one other person, preferably more. A child needs a chance to grow, not only physically, but emotionally and intellectually, to gratify his or her curiosity and wonder about the world. We call this a cosmic sense, a sense of identity and a sense of importance in one's self which one first

learns by being important to a few people: one's family and school, church and friends; small groups where one is an essential person, in which somebody would mind, someone would notice, "if you weren't there."[18]

The church is the special place to nurture the intuitive side of our being. Spirituality is the expression of the spirit, the intuitive, the deep passions, and our capacity for wonder, awe, and transcendence. Dorothy Arnett Dixon contends that spirituality is "a response which is more felt than thought, more intuitive than rational, more subconscious than conscious, and more 'of the soul' than of the mind."[19] We cannot give another spirituality, just as we cannot make another religious; but we can share our own spiritual depths and hunger, and provide occasions when the intuitive side of our being is enhanced and enlarged. Every service of worship has the potential for us to discover our openness and the range of the intuitive within us.

As educators, catching or being present during the teachable moment is crucial. For instance, when a child or adult catches hold of an idea, let us focus on it and celebrate it; or when a young person finds a colleague in the Bible or in a piece of devotional literature, let us remember to lift up that person. Dorothy Dixon pinpoints that teachable moment:

> Spirituality is the shriek of joy that the child emits while dancing with balloons and silken scarves. Spirituality is the burst of enthusiasm with which a child blows dandelion fuzz high into the air. Spirituality is the intense moment of awe and wonder expressed in silence as a child beholds a caterpillar on the sidewalk or a candle glowing in a special celebration.[20]

The Church's Worship Curriculum

Education in the church is a planned venture, and we need to be highly intentional about it as we answer the who, what, where, how, why, and when questions. This is particularly true when teaching people about worship. It is important to remember that we *do* learn to worship and we can be taught to worship.

Worship is part of the being and the doing of the church. Our experience in worship teaches us about God, the gospel, our neighbors, and ourselves. What is being learned through participation in the worship life of the congregation should be analyzed week in and week out. Is it what is intended? Is it all that is possible within the worship forms? In fact, churches of the Orthodox tradition work on the premise that the liturgy is *the* educative experience.

In addition to a planned curriculum, every environment, including the life of the congregation, has its "hidden curriculum," meaning it teaches without credentials, it buys no books, but it teaches nonetheless. Much of the medium's message is in tone, ethos, and style. Is our environment friendly to the spirit? Do people share important events in their life? Do people discuss problems? Do people ever mention Jesus? Do people touch when they greet one another? Are people only talked about behind their backs? Is it a place where people express a wide variety of emotions or only the polite ones? If the hidden curriculum is negative, very often it undermines the efforts of our planned curriculum. Obviously, if it is positive, it has a reinforcing effect.

A major part of education's role in relationship to worship is to offer an arena for serious discussion concerning the shape of worship. Part of its task is to ask what is appropriate to our lives as a Christian people and part of its task is to sort, analyze, and evaluate what other people have done. Many times worship patterns are divisive and controversial because they are imposed unilaterally or do not emerge from the struggling life of the whole congregation. The educational arena is the place to learn about the history, meaning, and forms of worship, and maybe to experiment with and practice a few.

Most denominationally produced curricula include instruction in worship history and practice, as well as resources for worship within the educational setting. Such resources include materials on the sacraments and on the Christian year. Usually these materials are quite good, and they may fall exactly on the button for the ages and subjects appropriate for young and old in the congregation. As a congregation, you need to be quite clear about which emphases you want to have made to which age groups and in which order. Utilize the resources of your denominational curriculum, but make it fit into your long-term worship/education strategy, and supplement such material when necessary.

The creative life of the congregation can be organized around special events and seasons. Wreaths and banners can be prepared for Advent, loving letters can be written for Valentine's Day, good luck wishes exchanged on St. Patrick's Day, and flowers shared at Easter. A birthday party can be readied for Pentecost and a Sukkoth booth can be built for Thanksgiving.[21] Each of these can be an organizing event for the whole congregation, involving education, activity, worship, fellowship, and mission. Other projects could entail some form of giving to others—baking cookies for Christmas, collecting an offering for racial justice on Martin Luther King's birthday, attending a work camp during Holy Week, supporting an environmental group during Trinity season, and contributing to Neighbors in Need or Native American ministries during the fall season.

An exciting project was undertaken by a congregation that took the parable of the talents seriously. Each person who chose to participate was given $5 and was asked to invest it in order to increase the money by using his or her individual talents. The money, given in January, was to be returned at a Sunday service in July. From time to time the church newsletter reported what was happening to the money—items made and sold, services rendered, stock market played, gardens cultivated, music performed, and tickets to benefit performances made available. One enterprising monotonic singer charged people a fee to keep him from singing. A group in the congregation sponsored a concert as a moneyraiser. At the ingathering it was learned that the original money had multiplied tenfold.

Another way to organize the life of a congregation is around a lectionary, where scripture readings are selected for each week of the year. The Sunday worship service, a business meeting, the fellowship group, and mission life can be related to the scripture text of the week. The churches of Australia and of New Zealand have formalized such an approach in a program called *Growing Together*.[22]

It is important for churches to be intentional about the teaching function as it relates to Sunday worship. You might try the experiment of setting aside one Sunday primarily as a teaching/learning Sunday, using the other Sundays in the month for a full worship expression. Or a one-and-a-half- to two-hour pattern could be established, with the first period designated for learning and related projects, and the second full hour for worship.

Many churches that have morning worship and church school at the same hour invite the children to share in the beginning of the worship service before they go to classes. This has the advantage of enabling children to come to the worship service with parents or friends and to get a taste of the worship experience that is reasonably consistent with their attention span. The disadvantages are that they do not get the full flow of the worship rhythm, and their time for study is extremely limited.

A children's sermon is often part of the worship. It normally belongs in the acceptance part. Perhaps the primary thing that happens here is that a person who is considered important conveys to children that they are special and that someone cares about them. The children are called forward to the chancel steps or other appropriate place where they can gather in a group around the storyteller.

To be effective, a *children's* sermon needs to be created with them in mind; it should not be a summary of the full sermon or an indirect statement to adults.

As you plan the children's sermon, take into account the developmental stages reviewed at the beginning of this chapter. Plan with a single, simple theme. Do not be abstract, since the ability of young children to generalize is very limited. Use stories of animals, concrete events, or everyday parables to make your point. Ask yourself, "What one thing do I want the children to do or remember?" Then develop your brief comments to make that happen.

Children's sermons are part of the worship whether the children stay through the whole service or not. A better pattern than having them leave with a truncated experience of both education and worship is to plan occasional intergenerational worship services that involve the full worship rhythm. The challenge to create a service that speaks to diverse age groups is real enough, but worship is meant to be expressive of the yearnings and faith of the whole church constituency.

Teaching Elements in a Worship Curriculum

Part of being intentional about education and worship is planning for ways in which the components of worship may be learned by members of the congregation. Some of this will vary by age level. Denominational curriculum materials and the stages material earlier in this chapter suggest some variations appropriate to given ages and stages in life.

There are eleven areas that, taken together, comprise the vertebrate structure of a worship curriculum for a church. The first element is *to explore the rhythm of worship.* Note especially the review of these elements in chapter 2 and suggestions for their expression in movement in chapter 8. Emphasis should be upon experience with the elements of adoration, confession, acceptance, and response. Choose a mode-of-the-month, and write prayers to express that mode. Do keep in mind, though, that the modes should not consistently be kept separate from one another. The rhythm is whole as life is whole, and each of the modes depends upon the others for completeness.

Specific attention needs to be given to practices related to offering and the use of money. The offering is one specific form of our response in worship that even the youngest child is capable of doing in some form. Monies should be physically carried to the offering plate by the givers and should be released as an act of self-giving. As part of the act we might interpret where the money goes, reflect upon the notion of grace, or define the doctrine of stewardship. One church prepares a day-by-day calendar for each month suggesting reasons for giving a nickel or a quarter. Another church has a "Hunger Month" emphasis, with a similar listing for each day.

The second component is *to understand the environment of worship*. This involves being able to recognize what you see and call it by its correct name. It includes awareness of the fixed symbols used in architectural form and the emergent symbols that are created in banners and in week-by-week worship life. Do on-the-spot teaching in the churches of your town. A scavenger hunt is a terrific form in which to help people come to know their worship environment. You can do it only in your own church or include neighboring ones as well.

The third element is *to share in the seasons of the Christian life*. The church year reflects diverse moods of the spirit. Our education is geared to help us participate in those days and their celebration, as well as to understand those dimensions in our own experience. The church year focuses upon Jesus' own pilgrimage and is an important resource for understanding his life, teaching, death, and resurrection. Our "seasoning" also relates to developmental stages in our life; therefore, educational effort needs to address these stages in faith experience and self-understanding.

The fourth dimension is *to meet the saints and the great literature of the Christian tradition*. The focus of this root work is on the worship experience of the Christian family through the ages. Some hymns and prayers now in use go back more than a thousand years. Persons like Augustine, Francis of Assisi, Julian of Norwich, and Saint Theresa provide deep insights into Christian experience. Devotional literature such as *The Little Flowers* of Francis of Assisi, Pascal's *Pensees*, Thomas Kelly's *A Testament of Devotion*, or John Baillie's *A Diary of Private Prayer* are important companions for today's journey.

Another dimension is *to enjoy the worship leadership of the congregation*. Often the pastor and the church musicians are experienced as being off in the distance somewhere doing their thing. We need to experience their sense of worship and gain insights into what makes them tick; we need to see them as live, passionate human beings. The interview process should be highly intentional and systematic, and should be set in the framework of a two-way dialogue.

A sixth element is *to practice prayer*. A great devotional classic is Brother Lawrence's *Practice of the Presence of God*.[23] Because praying is both spontaneous and learned, our education should enhance and encourage our spontaneity and our need to learn to pray by praying. Through our educational effort we need to learn the structure of praying and be in touch with patterns of prayer in diverse cultural situations. Prayer, in its private and corporate dimensions, is an important part of our learning. Students should begin developing a journal in which they write prayers and other thoughts they wish to keep as a centering part of their lives.

Another element is *to learn to sing hymns*. A very young child can learn to appreciate hymn tunes that he or she may sing throughout life. Much of the history of our tradition can be conveyed musically. Teaching about hymnody should also give us experience in hymn-writing and in swapping various tunes and texts.

An eighth dimension is *to participate in the forms of our faith*. This involves the creeds and the statements of faith that are some of the packages in which faith has been wrapped. The metaphor reminds us that the faith experience is fundamental, and that we will need to learn how to give expression to our own credos. This dimension includes getting in touch with symbolic words of the Christian faith—for instance, sin, forgiveness, communion, salvation, resurrection, faith, hope, love, and mission.

Let us remember that words are symbols representing reality. They can include or exclude. They can nurture or cripple. The National Council of Teachers of English, in defining guidelines for teaching and usage, says that

> language plays a central role in socialization, for it helps teach children the roles that are expected of them. Through language, children conceptualize their ideas and feelings about themselves and their world. Thought and action are reflected in words, and words in turn condition how a person thinks and acts.[24]

Many churches are using a learning center approach to education that is usually intergenerational. A theme or themes are chosen for the day, and activities are available in different centers. Emphases for the learning center may be chosen for a month at a time. For example, the listing below, spanning a twelve-month period, shows the programming of themes related to elements of faith.

September — Creation
October — Communion
November — Thanksgiving
December — Incarnation or Advent
January — Renewal
February — Penitence
March — Passion
April — Resurrection
May — Remembrance
June — Spirit
July — Freedom
August — Sabbath

The ninth component is *to share in sacraments and sacramentals.* Enormous teaching potential exists around special services like baptism, communion, confirmation, marriage, and ordination. Such services are usually more activity- and participatory-oriented than others. They touch key moments of life pilgrimages. We can trace central themes of the Christian life because they go way back in the church's history. Baptism touches cleansing, death and resurrection, grace and faith. Communion deals with sacrifice, solidarity, nurture and survival, betrayal and trust, and continuing love. Confirmation expresses faith, tithing, and belonging. Marriage affirms the mystery of one flesh, the meaning of covenant, and the stake of the community in the caring of people for one another. Ordination honors the vocation of each of us and the leadership power of the community of faith.

The tenth element is *to create liturgy.* Our education is not just to participate in somebody else's ideas; it is a time to create our own liturgical material. This involves creating orders of worship, responsive readings, calls to worship, prayers, hymns, and meditative material.

The final component is *to participate in leading liturgy.* If liturgy is to be the work of all the people, we must learn how to be one of these people. Our education should give us the experience of leading worship both in the educational setting and in the sanctuary. Whether our role is large or small to begin with, we can express ourselves as actors in the theatre of the spirit. One central element in worship leadership is helping people move from being spectators to being actors.

Principles of How Change Happens

Neither the status quo nor change are values in themselves. If we remember this, it will help us avoid unnecessary lethargy or change for change's sake. Liturgy is the work of the people, and the forms we choose should be those that work for us. This involves careful evaluation of what should be kept and what changed, and why.

Days and seasons change; events force themselves onto our calendar; lots of us have ideas that we want to try. Thus, our efforts to plan and lead worship will inevitably force us to make substantial changes in what we're doing. We want to maximize the effect of these changes. This section is addressed to that end as we consider the patterns and processes of change.

At the outset we must have clarity about our purpose. A great deal of change will be understood and supported when its purpose is clear. This involves affirmation of what is unchanged, as well as of the new. Some patterns we will keep because they fit our purposes, and some we will develop fresh, as a means of fulfilling our purposes.

The experiences that people have with worship are crucial. If, over a period of time, we have done a good job of helping people understand worship elements and their rationale, changes will happen easily, as new ideas and their rationale are developed. It will also help if people trust the judgment of their leadership and have a sense that they will have voice in patterns that are chosen to express their worship.

At the center of planning for change is the pastor and the professional staff. He, she, or they may be perceived as the "problem" by lay church members who want change. Insecurity, lack of experience with alternatives, or the comfortableness of doing things a particular way may all be factors in keeping the status quo. Worship, after all, is the pastor's "thing," and she or he has a life and professional stake in how it happens.

On the other hand, lay members may be perceived by the professional staff as centers of resistance to change. "They like things the way they have been," or, "They like the old hymns," or, "We tried something new once and everybody griped about it."

This we-they mentality has got to go. Liturgy is the work of all the people. What happens in a worship event is everyone's business. We're all onstage in the theatre of the spirit.

So, let us begin with the assumption that people are *not* the problem. The problem is how to design worship that helps us celebrate and express our spirituality and excites both God and us. Enthusiasm is the word with Greek New Testament roots that undergirds our understanding of spirit and the spirit itself.

A good sense of history helps. Most things we want to do have a precedent somewhere in the church's history: for instance, the psalms, whether said or sung, predate the writing of the Bible; dance was part of the worship from the times of Moses, Miriam, and David; a wide variety of instruments were used to praise God; the church, for centuries, was the patron of the arts, and church-sponsored theatre flourished in marketplace and sanctuary; for hundreds of years church architecture created the norms for the discipline; painting and sculpture were gifts used by artists through all of human existence to express religious meaning and serve as a form of holy offering; Luther perfected the practice of taking tunes from the marketplace and the tavern and, with appropriate words, bringing them into the sanctuary; and colonial New England churches were called meetinghouses, suggesting their open-door policy to concerns of the town and of the faith.

The term liturgy illustrates the importance of knowing the historical roots. Doug Adams describes the origins of the term which

> had an established meaning in the Greco-Roman world before the appearance of Christianity. At first it referred to the few days each year that the people would give (in lieu of or in addition to taxes) to build and repair the roads and bridges and other public works for the growth of the community. Later the term was applied to public service and servants of the gods. In calling their worship liturgy, Christians identified the purpose of their worship as a public service to God to build the community in particular shapes informed by word and sacrament.[25]

Thus, to give liturgy a tilt toward the world's concern is not to change the ground rules but, rather, to recover original meanings.

Another example of history and change is the black, large-sleeved Geneva gown worn by most clergy. John Calvin first wore this style of robe when he was a pastor in Geneva, Switzerland. It was the same garb worn by students and faculty at nearby University of Geneva. Its purpose was to symbolize the identification of clergy and laity. Today, however, worshipers experience the wearing of the gown as a mark of separation or distinction. Thus, if we want to cast aside the Geneva gown for street clothes or different vestments, history is on our side.

To deal with changing worship patterns effectively we need to find a "we" structure, in contrast to a "we-they" pattern, in which to do our worship planning. A worship committee can encourage worship planning in various segments of the church's life—church school, youth groups, men's and women's groups, business meetings, special celebrations—in order to develop a particular style and ethos that says, "Worship is everybody's business." Together we need to find the best ways to express our intentions and purposes. The following principles can help us do this creatively and with strong participation from the congregation:

The first principle is *to take careful inventory* of the rituals that are currently extant. Then find out why they exist and who are the people who want them to continue. Seek answers to such questions as, How did they get that way? Why have they stayed that way? What do people perceive to be right and good about the present? What are the differing views? Notice if the actual ritual patterns differ in description from what actually happens within them. Ask questions in an unbiased manner so as not to arouse suspicions. This inventory is primarily aimed at sorting out what happens that has value to people and what just happens.

The second principle is *to be clear about proposed changes.* What will be the same and what will be different? How will the new modify the old and vice versa? Who will be responsible for implementation?

Clarity may be hard in a participatory process, but take the time needed for people to air their views and then to focus in clearly on the subject at hand and the various alternatives being proposed.

The third principle is *to develop a careful strategy for change.* Will all the changes come at once? Will there be transitional or experimental stages? Who will be affected by the changes, and how will they have opportunity to deal with their effects? Who will monitor the changes to determine whether they are working?

John P. Kotter and Leonard A. Schlesinger offer advice on "Choosing Strategies for Change."[26] They describe variables that must be taken into account by the planners of change: What amount and type of resistance is anticipated? What is the position of the initiators with regard to trust and power in relationship to those who may resist? Who has the data for designing the change, and who is likely to provide the needed energy to implement the change? What are the stakes involved, and who are the stakeholders?

Our change strategies relate to all these questions and their answers. Other issues are those of timing and the relationship to natural groups in the church and to the processes of communication and interpretation. While communication is essential, normally a big publicity blast is not a good idea; either it will alarm people about the scope of change or it will increase expectations that the new forms do not meet. Without tricking people, it is better to experience forms in a natural way. People are seldom turned off by authentic worship, even if they are unfamiliar with it. But they are almost immediately turned off if they feel they are being toyed with or if they see themselves as the victims of insincerity.

Any strategy for change needs to provide for both feedback and corrective action. Although a clear timetable is important, it should be modifiable in the light of experience. The more people who are in on the strategy, the more likely it is to be effective. This does not mean that everyone has to help think it up, but that those affected should share in its shaping, implementing, evaluation, and modification.

A fourth principle is *to establish clear responsibility* for the change. Who has the authority to make decisions? Who will be the change agent? Who will help people to move into the new patterns?

The "who" is seldom one individual. Generally, it is a leadership group or a committee. It often depends on the informal leaders in a congregation. One of the classic stories of innovation has to do with the introduction of hybrid corn. Instead of imposing it on the farmers, county agents related to the Department of Agriculture and the land grant agricultural colleges introduced these changes to the local innovators and got them to try the new approach. Innovators were then followed by the early adopters and then by others as the new approaches proved themselves.[27]

The fifth principle is *to analyze and address the likely patterns and sources of resistance.* People may resist because they don't feel in the know, because they do not trust the change agent, or because they do not like the changes.

The pattern of force-field analysis is a useful one in considering change and resistance. One determines which forces are going for us (as in a magnetic field) and which against us. The positive ones are built upon, and the negative ones are given attention so their big force may be blunted.

Some elements can go either way. For example:

Negative	Positive
Don't trust the change agent	Trust the change agent
Comfortable with the status quo	Uncomfortable with the status quo
No experience with the new	Positive experience with the new
Fear of change	Change is a friend
Don't like to take risks	Risk is heady and exciting
Don't see the point	The point is obvious
Pace of potential change too quick	Pace of potential change just right

Kotter and Schlesinger identify four bases for resistance: The first they call *parochial self-interest*—people "think they will lose something of value as a result." The second is labeled *misunderstanding and lack of trust*—"people also resist change when they do not understand its implications and perceive that it might cost them much more than they will gain." A third factor is *different assessments*—people "assess the situation differently than . . . those initiating the change and see more costs than benefits resulting from the change." The fourth basis is *low tolerance for change*—"people also resist change because they fear they will not be able to develop the new skills and behavior that will be required of them."[28]

Kotter and Schlesinger identify several methods for dealing with change, and in the chart found on page 163 they note when and how such patterns are used and what their advantages and disadvantages are.[29]

Remember, these authors are writing about a business situation, not a voluntary association; nonetheless, their analysis is insightful. As we address each of these bases, keep in mind the pace of change, the leadership of change, and the value of change. One church has an annual hymnsing and potluck supper that's fun and provides two options: sing old favorites and learn some new ones. That is the best of both worlds and a good agent for change.

A sixth principle is *to establish an ongoing evaluative process,* so the new doesn't quickly become the new orthodoxy. As things go along, a consistently important element is interpreting what is going on. The church bulletin and newsletter can provide background on music, scripture, forms, and seasons. A hymn or scripture can be introduced with a parenthetical comment. Create a semiannual feedback sheet so that people can have input, demonstrating that the liturgy is indeed the work of all the people.

Methods for Dealing with Resistance to Change

Approach	Commonly Used in Situations	Advantages	Drawbacks
Education + communication	Where there is a lack of information or inaccurate information and analysis.	Once persuaded, people will often help with the implementation of the change.	Can be very time-consuming if lots of people are involved.
Participation + involvement	Where the initiators do not have all the information they need to design the change, and where others have considerable power to resist.	People who participate will be committed to implementing change, and any relevant information they have will be integrated into the change plan.	Can be very time-consuming if participators design an inappropriate change.
Facilitation + support	Where people are resisting because of adjustment problems.	No other approach works as well with adjustment problems.	Can be time-consuming, expensive, and still fail.
Negotiation + agreement	Where someone or some group will clearly lose out in a change, and where that group has considerable power to resist.	Sometimes it is a relatively easy way to avoid major resistance.	Can be too expensive in many cases if it alerts others to negotiate for compliance.
Manipulation + co-optation	Where other tactics will not work or are too expensive.	It can be a relatively quick and inexpensive solution to resistance problems.	Can lead to future problems if people feel manipulated.
Explicit + implicit coercion	Where speed is essential, and the change initiators possess considerable power.	It is speedy, and can overcome any kind of resistance.	Can be risky if it leaves people mad at the initiators.

A seventh principle is *to use clear-cut examples and rationale for proposed changes*. Ann Squire graphically points up the problem of language by offering two versions of the same paragraph. The original text reads:

> God is not glorified by the denigration of man, or by having man abased before him. On the contrary he is glorified as man attains a being more fully conformed to the image of God. . . . If worship is to fulfill our humanity it must bring man into his dignity as a spiritual creature. It must be liberating and enhancing.[30]

Squire translates the same text in these words:

> God is not glorified by having anyone debased. On the contrary God is glorified when men and women become more fully conformed to the image of God. If worship is to fulfill our personhood it must bring us—both male and female—into a sense of dignity as spiritual creatures. Worship must be liberating for both men and women.[31]

See how simple it is. The Squire version is more readable and certainly more inclusive. Someone reading this version would not know anything had been changed. Anyone with sensitivity reading the original would sense its limitations.

Ronald Kurtz worked on changed language through an educational process. On a sabbatical leave he studied biblical language. He wanted to know how to overcome what he felt were its sexist expressions. He concluded his study by stating seven guidelines that work for him:

1. If a reference is to God, say "God," not "he" or "she."
2. Speak of God with biblical words such as: "Yahweh," "Creator," "Holy One," "Sustainer."
3. If a reference is to a specific person, use the appropriate personal pronoun, "he" or "she."
4. If a reference is not to a specific person, use words that are inclusive, like "we," "they."
5. If a reference is to more than one person, and the group is not specifically designated as male or female, use words that are inclusive of both.
6. If a reference is to parent or ancestor, use words that include both male and female forbears.
7. Carefully read each passage to be used, compare translations, consult a Bible dictionary, then re-state . . . any unnecessarily sexist references.[32]

These changes are most effective if they grow out of the lives of people rather than seem to be imposed upon them by a worship leader. Who can quarrel with a member of the congregation who writes new words for an old tune? Who will resist a biblical translation carefully reworked and owned by an adult education class or a women's group? Who will quarrel with the language used in a worship service that a confirmation class or a men's group has developed to express its sense of the meaning of the Christian life?

These principles for dealing with change are tried and true. They do work. But they are exercised in the midst of the dynamic life of a group of worshiping people. Trust that life—its openness and its commitments. At the heart of this searching for relevant language and form is trust in the God who meets us in the midst of that searching. The Spirit is the supreme change-agent shaping people and forms to be agents of new life and promise.

Afterword

If you have traveled this far with us, you know how we have sought to explore the meaning of worship from a whole life perspective. We are called to love God with our heart, mind, soul, and strength. Pascal said that "the heart has reasons that reason does not know."[1] Worship is an affair of the *heart*, an expression of trusting, loving relationships between us and our neighbors and God. Worship is an expression of the *mind*—its imagination, believing, and sense of the logic of things. Worship is a dimension of the *soul*—the breath of life, the deep places, the intuitive qualities, the capacity for spirituality. Worship is an embodiment of our *strength*; our bodies are to be temples of God and we are to be members one of another.

The psalmist teaches us that we are to praise God with trumpet, lute, harp, tambourine, dancing, flute, strings, and cymbal. We are to express our faith, too, with language, environment, Bible, music, dance, education, and faithful action. Liturgy is the work of the people as that touches the whole of our lives. Robert Spike posed an interesting question when he spoke of our long-standing notion that worship is a preparation for life:

> May it not be that life is a preparation for worship? That is, that the daily deed of earning bread and the holy deed of waiting upon the Lord in company with his church flow in together. One is not rehearsal for the other. The worship of the Christian church must have this sturdiness about it that comes from a frequent mixture of the earthly problems of life with the promises of the Most Holy God.[2]

That mixture of life and promise is caught up in the rhythm of worship, a rhythm we have learned to express over the centuries of human experience with life and with God. Our capacity for wonder, awe, and adoration is God-given. Our yearning to express it is deep and signals the beginning of worship.

For our sins of omission and commission we seek forgiveness for

166

what we have been and done and for what we have never been and never done. Our sense of the not-yet-ness of life is pervasive.

The sense of holy acceptance touches the core of our being, and we explore it as good news. As we accept that acceptance, our lives are renewed and our spirits are made whole.

The rhythm of worship leads inexhorably to faith's response. If we love, we want to show it; if we are accepted, we want to accept others; and if God has touched us with faith, we want to be faith-bearers to others. Loving acceptance has the disciple effect of sending us on our way as agents of love, peace, and justice.

This remarkable action takes place in what we have chosen to call the Theatre of the Spirit. We mean thereby to emphasize that God is the audience and we are the actors. Something is not done to or for us; instead we, with kindred pilgrims, do the work of loving, of celebrating, and of being. In the meaning of covenant, each seeks the other; therefore, audience and actor are interdependent as each seeks to be faithful to the other. There is a you, a me, and an us in all this that fosters mutual growth.

This book has tended to emphasize the church building as the stage for action in the Theatre of the Spirit. Happily, we worship a God whom walls cannot contain and who determines the place of acting and watching. In a sense, the Theatre of the Spirit is any place in which people who love one another and their God find ways to express their adoration, confession, acceptance, and response. To be an actor in such a theatre is a remarkable vocation! The curtain is open. Let the worship begin!

Rey O'Day
Edward A. Powers

Appendix

An Order of Worship[1]

ADORATION

Prelude
*Call to Worship
    Leader: Praise God all the nations!
    People: Extol God all peoples!
    Leader: For great is God's steadfast love toward us.
    People: And the faithfulness of God endures forever.
    Unison: Praise God!
*Hymn of Adoration: "Now Let Every Tongue Adore Thee"
(Bach)
    Now let every tongue adore Thee!
    Let all with angels sing before Thee!
    Let harps and cymbals now unite.
    All thy gates with pearl are glorious.
    Where we partake through faith victorious,
    With angels round thy throne of light.
    No mortal eye hath seen,
    No mortal ear hath heard
    Such wondrous things,
    Therefore with joy our song shall soar
    In praise to God for evermore.
Invocation
    O holy God, you are pure love and compassion. You have
sought us out as the recipients of your care. We come to you
as those seeking love. Receive our adoration, awe, and wonder
at the majesty of your love. Enable us to be your covenant
partners, through Jesus Christ our Lord who has taught us to
pray,

* Congregation standing

168

The Lord's Prayer[2]
  Our God in heaven,
    holy be your name,
    your kingdom come,
    your will be done
    on earth as in heaven.
  Give us today the bread we need.
  Forgive us our sins
    as we forgive
    those who sin against us.
  Save us in the time of trial,
    and deliver us from evil.
  For the kingdom, the power, and the glory
    are yours now and forever. Amen.
Choral Response
Responsive Reading
  Leader: O God, how full of wonder and splendor you are.
  People: I see the reflections of your beauty and hear the
    sounds of your majesty wherever I turn.
  Leader: Even the babbling of babes and the laughter of chil-
    dren spell out your name in indefinable syllables.
  People: When I gaze at the star-studded skies and attempt to
    comprehend the vast distances,
  Leader: I contemplate in utter amazement my Creator's con-
    cern for me.
  People: I am dumbfounded that you should care for me.
  Leader: And yet you have made me in your image; you have
    called me your child.
  People: O God, how full of wonder and splendor you are.
    Your name should be known in all the earth.
  Anthem

CONFESSION

  Call to Confession
    Our God is one who remembers our histories and our sins.
    Our God is one who hears our confessions, restores our
    dreams, forgives our sins, and calls us to be what we have
    not yet become. Let us wait in silence before the holy God.
  Period of Silence
  Prayer of Confession
    O God of expectation, we have failed you. We have done what

we would rather not have done and left undone that which we wished to do. We have not loved our neighbors as ourselves, or you with all our heart, soul, mind, and strength. With you there is forgiveness and we ask for it. Renew a right spirit within us, and send us on our way rejoicing.

Assurance of Pardon
God's love is expressed in the incarnation in Jesus. The God who makes all things new offers each of us forgiveness, renewal, and the birth of new dreams and possibilities.
Choral Response
Concerns of the Community
*Hymn: "All-knowing God, Whose Science Charts" (William W. Reid) Tune: Creation

All-knowing God, whose science charts
The path and purpose of each star,
Who showest us the laws and arts
That whirl the mighty worlds afar;
Endow the nations with new skill
To use thy truth for larger good;
Endow the people with new will
To make the earth one neighborhood.

Almighty God, whose hand hath driven
The ocean's fury, shaken hills,
Yet patient strength to each hath given
To break all shackles, right all ills;
Embolden with thy might, we pray,
The hosts who clear new roads to peace;
Fulfill their vision of that day
When terror, war, and strife shall cease.

All-loving God, who hatest naught
Of thy creation's thousand forms,
Who for our fellowship hast sought
Despite our spirit's rebel storms;
Enlarge our love, strike down our hate;
Thus may thy will be done on earth,
And love fulfill in every state
The promise made at Jesus' birth. Amen.[3]

ACCEPTANCE

 *Scripture
 (*At the conclusion of each reading say the following:*)
   Leader: This is the word of God.
   People: Thanks be to God.
 Prayers of Intercession and Thanksgiving
 Sermon
 Prayer and Response

OFFERING

 *Statement of Faith
   We believe in God, the Eternal Spirit, who is made known
     to us in Jesus our brother and to whose deeds we testify:
   God calls the worlds into being, creates humankind in the
     divine image, and sets before us the ways of life and death.
   God seeks in holy love to save all people from aimlessness
     and sin.
   God judges all humanity and all nations by that will of righ-
     teousness declared through prophets and apostles.
   In Jesus Christ, the man of Nazareth, our crucified and risen
     Lord,
   God has come to us and shared our common lot, conquering
     sin and death
   and reconciling the whole creation to its creator.
   God bestows upon us the Holy Spirit, creating and renewing
     the church of Jesus Christ, binding in covenant faithful
     people of all ages, tongues, and races.
   God calls us into the church to accept the cost and joy of
     discipleship,
   to be servants in the service of the whole human family,
   to proclaim the gospel to all the world and resist the powers
     of evil,
   to share in Christ's baptism and eat at his table,
   to join him in his passion and victory.
   God promises to all who trust in the gospel forgiveness of
     sins and fullness of grace,
   courage in the struggle for justice and peace,
   the presence of the Holy Spirit in trial and rejoicing,
   and eternal life in that kingdom which has no end.
   Blessing and honor, glory and power be unto God. Amen.[4]

(If communion is included in the service, it begins here with the offering of gifts and communion elements.)

Offertory or Anthem
Offering
*Doxology
Praise God from whom all blessings flow,
Praise God, all creatures here below,
Praise God above the heavenly host,
Praise Creator, Christ, and Holy Ghost. Amen.
*Dedicatory Prayer
*Hymn of Dedication: "We Are One in the Spirit"
Benediction
Leader: The Lord be with you.
People: And also with you.
Leader: May Almighty God bless you, the Creator and Redeemer, and Sanctifier.
People: Amen.
Leader: Go in the peace of Christ.
People: Thanks be to God.
*Passing of the Peace
Postlude (congregation is asked to be seated for the postlude).

A Celebration of Personhood[5]
by the
Women's Task Force
Southern California Conference of
the United Church of Christ

Believe it,
You are a real find,
a joy in someone's heart.
You're a jewel,
unique and priceless.
I don't care how you feel.
Believe it,
God don't make no junk.

OUR COMMON CELEBRATION

WE ARE INVITED TO CELEBRATE
  Music to enjoy
  The invitation to celebrate
      Leader: Who do you think you are?
      People: We are the Church of Jesus Christ.
      Leader: What are you doing here?
      People: We have gathered here to remember what it means to be
               a person, a Christian, and a church.
      Leader: Will you be honest during this hour?
      People: We will try to be honest.
      Leader: Will your minds and hearts be open to God's Word?
      People: We will try to be open to God's Word.
      Leader: Good. Then we can proceed. Let us praise the God who
               is Creator of all things and all humanity.
  We sing "God of All Creation's Beauty," (Grace Moore) tune:
      Austrian Hymn

      God of all creation's beauty,
      Praise to you for change we see.
        Nothing fear we, though change scares us,
        You are not a God of fear.
          Now we celebrate our freedom
          To lead fully human lives.
            Glory, glory, ours the freedom;
            We rejoice in our personhood.

      Help us, Lord, to share our freedom
      By the way we live our lives.
        You have given us potential
        To reflect your holy self.
          Thru our own determined fulfillment
          May your love shine in our lives.
            Glory, glory, ours the knowledge;
            All are equal in your sight.

      May we heralds be for you Lord,
      Spread your gospel far and wide;
        That as your creation we are freed
        To be new persons in Christ.

* Congregation standing

There is no respect as to what race,
Economics, station, sex.
Glory, glory, yours the glory
Praise we our Creator God! Amen.[6]

Our prayer of adoration and confession
   Leader: Let us expose ourselves before the Lord of History.

Let us speak of our sin.

Beloved in the Lord, we have been given life, but we have not lived. We have been called to freedom, but we have found the burden heavy, the anxiety painful, and have returned to our illusions about life and our deceits about ourselves. Let us admit what is really within our lives; for when we do, it will be given back to us with brand new meaning and with hope.

All: Lord God, our Sustainer and Creator, we, your living Church, have paid lip service to our Christian beliefs and creeds.

We have been deceived into believing that what one spiritually believes is not really important . . .

Just as long as she or he retains some notion of what Christianity is about.

Lord, our heritage has been confessional . . . filled with a treasury of significant doctrines.

Yes, some of them need renewal in language and understanding yet their spiritual messages never change.

Lord forgive us,

for discrediting you as the Creator and Sustainer of all life,

for stripping the humanity from Christ's divinity and obscuring the divinity from Jesus's humanity,

for imprisoning the Holy Spirit in our ivory tower idealism,

for converting the universal Church into the inclusiveness of pettiness and apathy,

for breaking down the fellowship of the saints into a community of harmless puppets,

for replacing the forgiveness of sins with the pride of human achievement,

for forfeiting eternal life for transient pleasures and luxuries.

Stir our consciences with the guilt of our failings.
Comfort us with love.
Overcome us with the grace of Jesus Christ.
Right: Spirit of life and love, come to us and fill us;
Left: Spirit of growth and grace, come like a wind and
cleanse us;
Right: Come as a fire to burn.
Left: Stab us awake to reality.
Leader: Caught up in the common humanity of Christ's advanc-
ing purpose, let us rise and sing with the whole body.

　　*Praise God from whom all blessings flow,
　　Praise God, all creatures here below,
　　Praise God above ye heavenly hosts,
　　Praise God, and Christ, and Holy Ghost. Amen.

WE HEAR GOD'S WORD
Parable: The Lamp and the Bushel, Galatians 3:28:
"There is neither Jew nor Greek, there is neither slave nor free,
there is neither male nor female, for you are all one in Christ
Jesus."
Shared thoughts, concerns and announcements for the day
Thank Offering
*All share in Prayer:
Eternal Spirit in Heaven,
May everything praise you,
　may everyone acknowledge and obey you,
　may your purpose be achieved on earth as in heaven.
Give us each day what we need,
　one day at a time
　and forgive us the wrongs we have done
　as we forgive those who have wronged us.
Guide us away from temptation
　and release us from evil.
For you are the one who can do all this:
　nothing will ever overpower you
　and the highest honor is always yours.
So be it, Lord!
Children's Sermon: "Housework" and "My Dog Is a Plumber"
*We sing, "Rise Up, People of God" (from *Free to Be You and Me*)
Rise up, people of God!
Have done with lesser things;

Give heart and soul and mind and strength
To serve the King of kings.

Lift high the cross of Christ;
Tread where Christ's feet have trod;
As people of the risen Lord
Rise up, people of God!
Meditation: "New View of the Garden"
Prayer

WE RESPOND TO GOD'S WORD
Our Offering
*We sing, "Take My Life and Let It Be"
Take my life, and let it be consecrated, Lord, to thee;
Take my moments and my days, let them flow in ceaseless praise.

Take my hands, and let them move at the impulse of thy love;
Take my feet, and let them be swift and beautiful for thee.

Take my will, and make it thine; it shall be no longer mine;
Take my heart, it is thine own; it shall be thy royal throne.

Take my love: my Lord I pour at thy feet its treasure store;
Take myself, and I will be ever, only, all for thee. Amen.

*A Statement of Faith
We believe in God, the Eternal Spirit, one with our Lord Jesus
Christ and our Sustainer, and to the deeds of God we testify:
God calls the worlds into being,
creates humanity in the likeness of the Almighty
and sets before them the ways of life and death.
God seeks in holy love to save all people from
aimlessness and sin.
God judges people and nations with a righteous will
declared through prophets and apostles.
In Jesus Christ, the man of Nazareth, our crucified
and risen Lord,
God has come to us
and shared our common lot,
conquering sin and death
and reconciling the world to its creator.

God bestows upon us the Holy Spirit,
  creating and renewing the church of Jesus Christ,
  binding in covenant faithful people of all ages,
    tongues, and races.
Into God's church we are called
  to accept the cost and joy of discipleship,
  to be servants in the service of humanity,
  to proclaim the gospel to all the world
  and resist the powers of evil,
  to share in Christ's baptism
    and eat at the table of the Lord,
  to join in Christ's passion and victory.
To all who trust God is promised
  forgiveness of sins and fullness of grace,
  courage in the struggle for justice and peace,
  God's presence in trial and rejoicing,
  and eternal life in the kingdom of God which has no end.
Blessing and honor, glory and power be unto God. Alleluia![7]

*Leader: Do you sense the Lord's Presence within yours?
People: Yes, we do.
Leader: Then let us make a joyful noise unto the Lord.
    Praise the Lord with timbrel and dance.
People: Yes, for we are pilgrims in search of inspiration.
    We are children following a lord we call Christ.
    One who is: Lord of the dance,
          Lord of music,
          Lord of joy,
          Lord of life.
*We sing, "Lord of the Dance."

OUR PARTING WORDS OF LOVE
  *Friendship circle
  *Passing the peace
  *Benediction
    Leader: Our gathering will soon be ended;
        where will we go and what will we do?
    People: We will go out to be God's people in the world.
    Leader: May peace and joy forever accompany you. Amen.
    People: Amen.
  *Music to enjoy

A Service of Holy Communion[8]

THE THANKSGIVING

Celebrant: The Lord be with you.
    People: And also with you.
Celebrant: Lift up your hearts.
    People: We lift them to the Lord.
Celebrant: Lord, we thank you and praise you.
        Only you are God
        You created all things and called them good.
        You made us in your own image.
        Even when we rebelled against your love,
           you did not desert us.
        You delivered us from captivity,
           made covenant
           and spoke to us through your prophets.
    People: God, we thank you and praise you.
Celebrant: You loved the world so much that you sent
           your Son to be our Savior.
        The Lord of all life came to live among us.
        He healed and taught,
           ate with sinners,
           and won for you a new people
           by water and the Spirit.
        We saw his glory.
    People: God, we thank you and praise you.
Celebrant: At your command all things came to be: the vast expanse of interstellar space, galaxies, suns, the planets in their courses, and this fragile earth, our island home.
    People: By your will they were created and have their being.
Celebrant: From the primal elements you brought forth the human race, and blessed us with memory, reason and skill. You made us the rulers of creation. But we turned against you, and betrayed your trust; and we turned against one another.
    People: Have mercy, Lord, for we are sinners in your sight.
Celebrant: Again and again, you called us to return. Through prophets and sages you revealed your righteous Law. And in the fullness of time you sent your only Son, born of a woman, to fulfill your Law, to open for us the way of freedom and peace.

People: By his blood, he reconciled us.
By his wounds, we are healed.
Celebrant: And therefore we praise you, joining with the chorus of prophets, apostles and martyrs, and with all those in every generation who have looked to you in hope, to proclaim with them your glory, in their unending hymn.
People: Holy, holy, holy, God of hosts,
Heaven and earth are filled with your glory.
Hosanna in the highest.
Celebrant: Yet your Son humbled himself in obedience to your will;
He stretched out his arms upon the cross.
By dying, he freed us from unending death;
By rising from death he gave us eternal life.
And on the night he was arrested, in company with his close friends, the Lord Jesus took bread.
After giving thanks, he broke the bread and said.
This is my body, which is for you:
Do this, remembering me.
In the same way, he took a cup of wine after supper and said:
This cup is the new covenant
Sealed in my blood.
Whenever you drink it, do this,
Remembering me.

CONSECRATION

All: On the night that he was betrayed by one he trusted, utterly alone before the powers and principalities of civilization, he took up the bread of survival, and when he gave thanks, he broke it in the act of unconditional sharing—this is my body given for you. Inasmuch as you share with the least of these my friends, you share it with me.

After supper he took the wine of joy. And when he had given thanks, he gave it to them: This is my blood of the new age coming, shed for you and for many; drink this in promise and foretaste of when we shall drink it together in laughter.

THE WORD

An Offering of Poetry

People: Christ has died,
Christ has risen,
Christ will come again!

Celebrant: Remembering the Lord Jesus, we pray you to send the power of your Holy Spirit upon us and upon this bread and wine, that we who receive the body and blood of Christ may be his Body in the world, living according to his example, announcing his death, and telling his resurrection to all peoples and nations.

People: Amen!

THE LORD'S PRAYER

Celebrant: As Jesus taught us, we pray:
People: Our God in heaven,
holy be your Name,
your kingdom come,
your will be done
on earth as in heaven.
Give us today the bread we need.
Forgive us our sins
as we forgive
those who sin against us.
Save us in the time of trial,
and deliver us from evil.
For the kingdom, the power, and the glory
are yours now and forever.
Amen.

THE BREAKING OF THE BREAD AND THE DRINKING OF THE CUP

Celebrant: Because there is one loaf,
we, many as we are, are one body;
for we all partake of the one loaf.

When we break the bread,
is it not a means of sharing
in the Body of Christ?

People: We are one;
this is the Body of Christ.

Celebrant: When we give thanks over the cup,
is it not a means of sharing
in the Blood of Christ?
People: We share in his Blood;
this is the Blood of Christ.
Celebrant: All is ready.
Come, let us share together.

* DISTRIBUTION OF THE ELEMENTS

(All who wish to share in the Communion are now invited to receive communion at one of the stations. Please move to the station closest to you. Both wine and grape juice are available at all stations. If you prefer, you may dip your bread in the common cup instead of drinking from it. Please share the bread and the cup freely with each other. The words of administration are:)

"The Body of Christ, broken for you."
Response: Amen.
"The Blood of Christ, shed for you."
Response: Amen.

During the distribution we will sing:
"Let Us Break Bread Together"
"Hearts Open Slowly"
"God Is Like a River Flowing"
"Amazing Grace"
"Kumbaya"

THE DEDICATION

Celebrant: You have given yourself to us, Lord.
People: Now we give ourselves for others.
Celebrant: Your love has made us a new people;
People: As a people of love we will serve you with joy.
Celebrant: Your glory has filled our hearts.
People: Help us glorify you in all things.
All: Amen.

THE PEACE

Celebrant: Since God loved us so much,
we too should love one another.
Let us share together signs and words of peace.
The peace of the Lord Jesus Christ be with us all.
People: Amen.

* Congregation standing

* Hymn
  "I'm on My Way"
* Dismissal
  Celebrant: Go. God's peace be with you.
  Live as free women and men rejoicing
  in the power of the Holy Spirit.
  People: We are God's people,
  sent in Christ's name.
  All: Thanks be to God!
* Benediction
* Hymn medley

Advent Service for the Home

The word Advent comes from the Latin words meaning "to come." The Advent season begins on the fourth Sunday before Christmas and ends on Christmas Eve. Its purpose is to anticipate the coming of the Christchild and to learn what it means that God loved humanity so much as to come to earth in human garb. Five candles (usually four purple, and a white one for Christmas Eve) are placed together, often in a wreath. They should remain in the same spot during the advent season. Each Sunday the candles previously lit are relighted before the service begins. The numbers in each service refer to a particular reader. From Sunday to Sunday family members should rotate so that persons have different numbers. It is a good idea to plan an activity or a giving project with each service.

FIRST SUNDAY

1. I light this candle to symbolize *hope.* As we begin our preparation for the birth of the Christchild, we remember Jesus' promise of hope.

All sing: "O Come, O Come, Emmanuel."

2. Read the Magnificat—Luke 1:46-55.
3. Help us to be kind to each other as we prepare for Christmas and enable us to understand Jesus' message of hope. Amen.

SECOND SUNDAY

1. *(Relight first candle.)* All the world wants *peace.* Jesus is God's

gift of peace to the world. To last week's candle of hope, we add one which tells of *peace*.
2. I light the second candle to symbolize the peace of which the Christmas angels sang.

All sing: "O Little Town of Bethlehem."

3. Read Isaish 11:1-9, the vision of the peaceable kingdom.
4. Help us, O God, to learn the ways of the Prince of Peace. Amen.

THIRD SUNDAY

1. (*Relight first two candles.*) These candles remind us of hope and peace. Tonight we light the third candle symbolic of love.

All sing: "What Child Is This?"

2. Read John 1:1-14.
3. Dear God, help us love you and love one another. Amen.

FOURTH SUNDAY

1. (*Relight first three candles.*) These candles remind us of hope, peace, and love. The candle we light tonight expresses the *joy* at the coming of Jesus into the world.

All sing: "Joy to the World."

2. Read Isaiah 9:6-7.
3. Dear God, help us find ways to share with others the good news of Jesus. Amen.

CHRISTMAS EVE

1. (*Relight the first four candles.*) These candles have helped us to think of Jesus as hope, peace, love, and joy. Tonight we celebrate his birth in a stable long ago in a faraway land.
2. Read Luke 2:1-20.
3. As we light our fifth candle, let us think about Jesus, the Light of the World, and what his coming has meant to all people everywhere.

4. As we look at all the candles glowing, we remember Christmas with joy and give thanks for God's love. Dear God, help us to keep Christmas in our hearts this night and throughout the year ahead. Through Jesus Christ our Lord. Amen.

All sing: "Silent Night."

Notes

CHAPTER 1 THE WORK OF THE PEOPLE

1. *The Unchurched American* (Princeton, N.J.: Princeton Religious Research Center and the Gallup Organization, Inc., 1978).
2. Evelyn Underhill, *Worship* (New York: Harper & Row, Torchbook, 1936), p. 3.
3. Paul S. McElroy, *Quiet Thoughts* (New York: Peter Pauper Press, 1964), pp. 10f.
4. Edward K. Perry, *Learning About Fishing in Upper New York*, Upper New York Synod, Lutheran Church in America, 1975, p. 10.
5. David A. Roozen, *Protestant Church Membership and Participation: Trends, Determinants, and Implications for Policy and Planning* (Hartford, Conn.: The Hartford Seminary Foundation, 1978), p. 55.
6. Phyllis Trible, *God and the Rhetoric of Sexuality* (Philadelphia: Fortress Press, 1978).
7. Sam Keen and Anne Valley Cox, *Telling Your Story: A Guide to Who You Are and Who You Can Be* (New York: Doubleday, 1973), p. 8.
8. John Marsh, *A Book of Public Worship* (London: Oxford University Press, 1949), p. ix.

CHAPTER 2 THE RHYTHM OF WORSHIP

1. Rachel Carson, *The Sense of Wonder* (New York: Harper & Row, 1956), pp. 42f.
2. Call to Worship used at a Sunday morning worship service at Judson Memorial Church, New York City. Used by permission of the Rev. Al Carmines.
3. Call to Worship from "A Booklet of Worship Aids," Commission on Evangelism and Worship, Indiana-Kentucky Conference, United Church of Christ, 1976. Used by permission.
4. *An Order of Worship*, Consultation on Church Union, 1968, p. 12. Used by permission.
5. This litany was used by the Rev. Ralph C. Unruh in the First Congregational Church, Jamestown, New York.
6. Litany adapted by the Rev. Frank Chong of Honolulu from *Na Himeni Haipule Hawaii*. Used by permission of Hawaii Conference Foundation.

7. This is a statement of common affirmations developed at a meeting of the Commission on Faith and Order of the National Council of Churches. While it was not meant for circulation, it has been found by some ecumenical groups to be of liturgical value, precisely for the reason which the Commission composed it. It is here used by permission.

8. United Church of Christ Statement of Faith. Adaptation by Robert V. Moss, Jr. Reprinted from *History and Program* (3d ed.; New York: United Church Press, 1978). Copyright © 1978 United Church Press.

9. *Woman-Soul Flowing, Words for Personal and Communal Reflection,* 1978, p. 24. Printed with permission of the Ecumenical Women's Center, 1653 W. School Street, Chicago, Illinois 60657.

10. Prayer used at a Sunday morning worship service at Judson Memorial Church, New York City. Used by permission of the Rev. Howard Moody.

11. Paul Tillich, "You Are Accepted," *The Shaking of the Foundations* (New York: Charles Scribner's Sons, 1948), p. 162.

12. *Woman-Soul Flowing,* op. cit., p. 11.

13. William B. Oden, *Liturgy as Life Journey* (Los Angeles: Acton House, 1976), p. 97.

14. Author unknown.

CHAPTER 3 FAITH AND FORM

1. Margaret Mead, as reported by Roger L. Shinn in "I Miss You, Margaret," *Christianity and Crisis,* December 11, 1978, p. 306.

2. Used in liturgy at the United Church of Christ National Meeting of Women, Cincinnati, January 12, 1979. Used by permission of the Advisory Commission on Women: United Church of Christ.

3. Dag Hammarskjöld, *Markings* (New York: Alfred A. Knopf, 1964); E. Stanley Jones, *The Way* (Nashville: Abingdon Press, 1946); Thomas R. Kelly, *A Testament of Devotion* (New York: Harper & Row, 1941); *The Daily Word* (Unity Village, Mo.: Unity School of Christianity).

4. Charles Francis Whiston, *Teach Us to Pray* (New York: Pilgrim Press, 1949).

5. Ibid., p. 125.

6. The Bible uses the word father in many places. The most intimate is Jesus' prayer in Mark 14:36 (see also Romans 8:15). Motherly attributes of God are expressed in such passages as Isaiah 66:13; Genesis 3:21; Isaiah 42:14; 49:15; Psalm 22:9-10; Jeremiah 31:20; and Deuteronomy 32:18.

7. Robert Bellah, *Beyond Belief: Essays on Religion in a Post-Traditional World* (New York: Harper & Row, 1970), p. 21.

8. Evelyn Underhill, *Worship* (New York: Harper & Row, Torchbook, 1936), p. 32.

9. *Webster's Third New International Dictionary of the English Language Unabridged* (Springfield, Mass.: G. & C. Merriam Co., 1961), p. 1497.

10. Krister Stendahl, "Enrichment or Threat? When the Eves Come Marching In," *Sexist Religion and Women in the Church: No More Silence!,* ed. by Alice L. Hageman (New York: Association Press, 1974), p. 120.

11. Rey O'Day, "Why All the Fuss About Language?" Copyright 1979. Research on God language done by NOW Task Force on Religion. Used by permission of the author.

12. Edward A. Powers, quoted from *Liberating Words, Images, and Actions—Guidelines to Alleviate Stereotyping,* p. 30. Copyright 1979 by the Joint Educational Development, 341 Ponce de Leon Avenue, N.E., Atlanta, Georgia 30308. Material used by permission.

13. Gwen Kennedy Neville and John H. Westerhoff III, *Learning Through the Liturgy* (New York: Seabury Press, 1978), p. 60.

14. Dom Gregory Dix, *The Shape of the Liturgy* (London: A. & C. Black Ltd.; reprinted 1975). Distributed in the United States by Christian Classics, 205 Willis Street, Westminster, Maryland 21157.

15. Benson Saler, "A Look at Ritual," *Liturgy,* Vol. 18, No. 1 (January 1973), p. 12.

16. *An Order for the Celebration of Holy Baptism,* Consultation on Church Union, 1973, pp. 31f. Used by permission.

17. From *Word and Table,* p. 14. Copyright © 1976 by Abingdon Press. Used by permission.

18. Ibid.

19. Excerpts from the English translation of the *Roman Missal* © 1973, International Committee on English in the Liturgy, Inc. All rights reserved. Used by permission.

20. From the International Consultation on English Texts, 1975 version. Used with permission.

21. Ibid.

22. Authorized for use by the Twenty-Third General Council of the United Church of Canada. Text slightly altered.

CHAPTER 4 SYMBOLS AND SEASONS OF THE CHRISTIAN YEAR

1. Herbert Ginsburg and Silvia Opper, *Piaget's Theory of Intellectual Development, An Introduction* (Englewood Cliffs, N.J.: Prentice-Hall, 1979), p. 1.

2. Drawing by Laura Bachwansky. Adapted from a diagram in *Christian Symbolism in the Evangelical Churches* by Thomas A. Stafford (Nashville: Abingdon Press, 1942), p. 138.

3. Stuart Hampshire, *New York Review of Books,* March 31, 1977.

4. Halford E. Luccock, "Let's Give Seven Yells!" *The Christian Century,* February 15, 1956. Reprinted in *A Sprig of Holly* (New York: Pilgrim Press, 1978), p. 43.

5. This listing is offered with thanks to Dr. Tari Lennon, Church of the Oaks, United Church of Christ, Thousand Oaks, California. Used by permission.

CHAPTER 5 ENVIRONMENT FOR WORSHIP

1. *Webster's Third New International Dictionary of the English Language Unabridged* (Springfield, Mass.: G. & C. Merriam Co., 1961), p. 760.

2. Ibid.

3. Samuel H. Miller, *The Dilemma of Modern Belief* (New York: Harper & Row, 1963), p. 37.

4. Edward A. Sovik, *Architecture for Worship* (Minneapolis: Augsburg Publishing House, 1973), p. 44.

5. Paul Goldberger, "A Place of Searching," *Journal of Current Social Issues*, Fall 1978, p. 51.

6. Ibid., pp. 51f.

7. Many denominations are giving extensive attention to the ease of access for handicapped persons to church buildings. Write to your denominational headquarters for information. See also *Modern Liturgy*, Vol. 4, No. 5 (P.O. Box 444, Saratoga, California 95070).

8. Sovik, *Architecture for Worship*, op. cit.

9. Mildred C. Widber and Scott Turner Ritenour, *Focus: Building for Christian Education* (New York: Pilgrim Press, 1969).

10. *Worship and the Arts*, a series of six multimedia kits. The Joint Worship Office, 1044 Alta Vista Road, Louisville, Kentucky 40205.

11. Douglas Hoffman, ed., *The Energy-efficient Church* (New York: Pilgrim Press, 1979).

12. Elizabeth Cogburn, "Do-It-Yourself Guide for Making Ceremonials," *Quest*, May-June 1978, p. 126.

13. Author unknown.

CHAPTER 6 THE BIBLE IN WORSHIP

1. *Nelson's Complete Concordance of the Revised Standard Version Bible* (New York: Thomas Nelson, Inc., 1978).

2. *The Interpreter's Dictionary of the Bible*, ed. by George A. Buttrick, four volumes (Nashville: Abingdon Press, 1962).

3. *The Interpreter's Bible*, twelve volumes (Nashville: Abingdon Press, 1951–54).

4. *The Anchor Bible*, multiple volumes (New York: Doubleday, 1974ff.).

5. Litany utilized at the United Church of Christ National Meeting of Women, Cincinnati, January 12, 1979. Used by permission of the Advisory Commission on Women: United Church of Christ.

6. For fuller treatment of the Genesis material on Adam and Eve, see Phyllis Trible, *God and the Rhetoric of Sexuality* (Philadelphia: Fortress Press, 1978). The journey of Abraham and Sarah is reported in Genesis 12:1-9. Abraham's potential sacrifice of Isaac is found in Genesis 22:1-18. The story of Deborah is found in Judges 4—5. The whole book of Esther makes exciting reading. The Red Sea crossing is to be found in Exodus 12:37—15:19. Miriam's dancing and song are described in Exodus 15:20-21.

CHAPTER 7 MUSIC IN WORSHIP

1. Quoted in Herbert A. L. Jefferson, *Hymns in Christian Worship* (New York: Macmillan, 1950), pp. 258f.
2. Personal comment to the authors. Used by permission.
3. The American Guild of Organists is at 630 Fifth Avenue, New York, New York 10020.
4. The Hymn Society of America is at Wittenberg University, Springfield, Ohio 45501.
5. Richard K. Avery and Donald S. Marsh, *The Avery and Marsh Songbook* (Port Jervis, N.Y.: Proclamation Productions, 1977).
6. "In Christ There Is No East or West" by John Oxenham. Used by permission of Theo Oxenham.
7. From *The Shalom Hymnal,* ed. by the Rev. Grace Moore (Long Beach, Calif.: R. & S. Printing Co., 1979), p. 20. Used by permission.
8. *Sing Shalom,* United Church Board for Homeland Ministries. Order from DECEE, P.O. Box 179, St. Louis, Missouri 63166, 1978; Sharon and Tom Neufer Emswiler, *Sisters and Brothers Sing,* The Wesley Foundation Campus Ministry, 211 N. School Street, Normal, Illinois 61761; *Because We Are One People,* (Chicago: Ecumenial Women's Center, 1974); *The Shalom Hymnal,* op. cit.
9. Albert C. Ronander and Ethel K. Porter, *A Guide to the Pilgrim Hymnal* (New York: Pilgrim Press, 1966).
10. H. Augustine Smith, *Lyric Religion: The Romance of Immortal Hymns* (Old Tappan, N.J.: Fleming H. Revell, 1931).
11. John Foley, "Music in the Mass: A Practical Approach," *Hosanna,* Phoenix, North American Liturgy Resources, December 1977, p. 12.
12. From "Inclusive Language Guidelines for Use and Study in the United Church of Christ."
13. Personal comment to the authors. Used by permission.
14. Adapted from a litany used by the Rev. Charles O. Erickson, The Congregational Church of Birmingham, Bloomfield Hills, Michigan. Used by permission.

CHAPTER 8 MOVEMENT IN WORSHIP

1. Carla de Sola, *The Spirit Moves, A Handbook of Dance and Prayer* (The Liturgical Conference, 810 Rhode Island Avenue N.E., Washington, D.C. 20018, 1977), p. 14. Used by permission.
2. Edwin Markham, "Outwitted," *The Best Loved Poems of the American People* (New York: Doubleday, 1936), p. 67. Used by permission.
3. Anne M. Squire, "Women and Spirituality," *Religious Education,* Vol. 72, No. 3 (May–June 1978), p. 325.
4. Isadora Duncan, *Art of the Dance* (New York: Theatre Arts).
5. Rey O'Day, "I Am a Dancer." Copyright 1979. Used by permission of the author.

CHAPTER 9 EDUCATIONAL DEVELOPMENT AND WORSHIP

1. Daniel J. Levinson, *The Seasons of a Man's Life* (New York: Alfred A. Knopf, 1978), p. 7.

2. Jean Piaget, *Six Psychological Studies* (New York: Random House, Vintage Book, 1967).

3. Lawrence Kohlberg, "Stage and Sequence: The Cognitive-Developmental Approach to Socialization," *Handbook of Socialization Theory and Research*, ed. by David A. Goslin (Chicago: Rand McNally, 1969), pp. 347–480; James Fowler and Sam Keen, *Life-Maps: Conversations on the Journey of Faith* (Waco, Tex.: Word Books, 1978); Erik Erikson, *Childhood and Society* (New York: W. W. Norton, 1964); Gwen Kennedy Neville and John H. Westerhoff III, *Learning Through Liturgy* (New York: Seabury Press, 1978); Gail Sheehy, *Passages* (New York: Bantam Books, 1977).

4. James Fowler, "Stages in Faith: The Structural-Developmental Approach," unpublished paper, September 1975, p. 20. Used by permission.

5. Bruno Bettelheim, *The Uses of Enchantment: The Meaning and Importance of Fairy Tales* (New York: Random House, 1977).

6. Fowler, "Stages in Faith," op. cit., p. 21.

7. Neville and Westerhoff, *Learning Through Liturgy*, op. cit., p. 162.

8. Fowler, "Stages in Faith," op. cit., p. 24.

9. Levinson, *The Seasons of a Man's Life*, op. cit., p. 57.

10. Fowler, "Stages in Faith," op. cit., pp. 25f.

11. Ibid., p. 13.

12. Levinson, *The Seasons of a Man's Life*, op. cit., pp. 197ff.

13. Carl Jung, *Man and His Symbols* (New York: Doubleday, 1964).

14. Levinson, *The Seasons of a Man's Life*, op. cit., p. 36.

15. Penelope Washbourn, *Becoming Woman: The Quest for Spiritual Wholeness in Female Experience* (New York: Harper & Row, 1977).

16. C. Ellis Nelson, *Where Faith Begins* (Atlanta: John Knox Press, 1967), p. 10.

17. James M. Gustafson, *The Church as Moral Decision-Maker* (New York: Pilgrim Press, 1970).

18. Margaret Mead, *Journal of Current Social Issues*, Winter 1978–79, p. 3.

19. Dorothy Arnett Dixon, "Spirituality, World Religions, and Education," *Religious Education*, May–June 1978, p. 345.

20. Ibid.

21. See Keith and Carolyn Boyer, *Harvest/Thanksgiving*, a Living the Word Resource published for "Christian Education: Shared Approaches" (New York: Pilgrim Press, 1979).

22. This program is under the auspices of the Joint Board of Christian Education of Australia and New Zealand, 177 Collins Street, Melbourne, Australia 3000.

23. Brother Lawrence, *The Practice of the Presence of God* (Old Tappan, N.J.: Fleming H. Revell, 1975).

24. *Guidelines for Nonsexist Use of Language* (Washington, D.C.: National Council of Teachers of English).

25. Doug Adams, "Free Church Worship and Sunday Work," *New Conversations*, Vol. 3, No. 3 (Winter 1978–79), p. 14.

26. John P. Kotter and Leonard A. Schlesinger, "Choosing Strategies for Change," *Harvard Business Review*, March–April 1979, pp. 112f. Copyright © 1979 by the President and Fellows of Harvard College; all rights reserved. Used by permission of the Harvard Business Review.

27. This process implemented congressional legislation enacted in 1914. The process is written up in two Iowa State College Agricultural Extension Service bulletins, No. 15 (dated November 1955) and No. 18.

28. Kotter and Schlesinger, "Choosing Strategies for Change," op. cit., pp. 107–9.

29. Reprinted by permission of the Harvard Business Review. Exhibit from "Choosing Strategies for Change" by John P. Kotter and Leonard A. Schlesinger (March–April 1979). Copyright © 1979 by the President and Fellows of Harvard College; all rights reserved.

30. John Macquarrie, *Paths in Spirituality* (New York: Harper & Row, 1972), p. 7.

31. Anne M. Squire, "Women and Spirituality," *Religious Education*, May–June 1978, p. 334.

32. Ronald Kurtz, "Seven Inclusive Tips to Re-state Scripture," *A.D.* magazine, March 1978, p. 60. Copyright 1978 *A.D.* Used by permission.

AFTERWORD

1. Blaise Pascal, *Pensees* (New York: E.P. Dutton, 1958).

2. Robert W. Spike, *In But Not of the World* (New York: Association Press, 1957), p. 54.

APPENDIX

1. "An Order of Worship" draws its call to worship from a February 26, 1977 service of worship sponsored by COMMIT (an organization that is no longer in existence) in Los Angeles.

2. The Lord's Prayer version is from the United Church of Christ National Meeting of Women, Cincinnati, January 12, 1979. Used by permission.

3. The hymn "All-knowing God, Whose Science Charts" by William W. Reid. Copyright 1958 by The Hymn Society of America. Used by permission.

4. United Church of Christ Statement of Faith. Adaptation by Robert V. Moss, Jr. Reprinted from *History and Program* (3rd ed.; New York: United Church Press, 1978). Copyright © 1978 United Church Press.

5. "A Celebration of Personhood" prepared by Rey O'Day for the Women's Task Force of the Southern California Conference of the United Church of Christ in Pasadena. Used by permission.

6. Words copyright 1973 by Grace Moore. Used by permission.

7. Adapted from the United Church of Christ Statement of Faith.

8. This communion service was first used at the United Church of Christ National Meeting of Women, Cincinnati, January 12, 1979. Used by permission.

Annotated Bibliography

CHAPTER 1 THE WORK OF THE PEOPLE

J.G. DAVIES, ed., *The Westminster Dictionary of Worship*. Philadelphia: Westminster Press, 1972. This dictionary-like work provides descriptive material on various worship and liturgical elements.

DOM GREGORY DIX, *The Shape of the Liturgy*. London: A. & C. Black, Ltd., reprinted edition, 1975. Distributed in the United States by Christian Classics, 205 Willis Street, Westminster, Maryland 21157. This is a classic work by an Anglican scholar who explores liturgy's shape as historically developed.

CHESLYN JONES, GEOFFREY WAINRIGHT, and EDWARD YARNOLD, eds., *The Study of Liturgy*. New York: Oxford University Press, 1978. The book contains a series of essays exploring historical and contemporary issues in the development of the liturgy, the sacraments, ordination, and the Christian year. Provides excellent historical background.

SAM KEEN and ANNE VALLEY COX, *Telling Your Story: A Guide to Who You Are and Who You Can Be*. New York: Doubleday, 1973. Provides an interpretation of the Bible as story and "my faith pilgrimage" as "my story."

EVELYN UNDERHILL, *Worship*. New York: Harper & Row, Torchbook, 1936. This is the classic treatment of the meaning of worship by the English mystic. She deals with worship as response of the creature to the Eternal and is particularly helpful in dealing with ritual, myth, and symbol.

JAMES F. WHITE, *Christian Worship in Transition*. Nashville: Abingdon Press, 1976. An analysis of recent directions in the field of worship theory and practice.

CHAPTER 2 THE RHYTHM OF WORSHIP

Exploring Worship in a Congregation. New York: Office for Church Life and Leadership, United Church of Christ, 1977. Order from

Box 179, St. Louis, Missouri 63166. Offers a packet with pockets full of background material to help a congregation plan for worship.

MURRAY J. FORD, *Planning, Preparing, Praising: Worship Resources for the Laity.* Valley Forge, Pa.: Judson Press, 1978. This is a brief collection of worship materials—prayers, calls to worship, and meditations. It includes some church year materials. The language is sexist.

HOYT HICKMAN, *Word and Table: A Basic Pattern of Sunday Worship for United Methodists.* Nashville: Abingdon Press, 1976. This booklet offers the recommended structure of worship for United Methodist congregations. Rationale is interpreted.

BARD THOMPSON, *Liturgies of the Western Church.* Cleveland: Collins-World, 1974. Provides a collection of liturgies of Lutheran, Reformed, and Anglican traditions in Europe and in the United States, with commentary on their history and constituent parts.

MIRIAM THERESE WINTER, *Preparing the Way of the Lord.* Nashville: Abingdon Press, 1978. The author of "Joy Is Like the Rain," Sister Miriam of the Medical Mission Sisters, describes the process of liturgical renewal, especially from within the Catholic tradition. A section of the book is devoted to helping groups develop liturgical forms.

Woman-Soul Flowing: Words for Personal and Communal Reflection. Ecumenical Women's Center, 1653 W. School Street, Chicago, Illinois 60657, 1978. This is a collection of meditations for devotional use. Includes several litanies and response prayers for corporate use. The book is handsome and nonsexist.

"Worship: Inclusive Language Resources." New York: Office for Church Life and Leadership, United Church of Christ, 1977. Order from Box 179, St. Louis, Missouri 63166. This booklet offers a variety of liturgical resources.

CHAPTER 3 FAITH AND FORM

MALCOLM M. BOYD, *Are You Running with Me, Jesus?* New York: Holt, Rinehart & Winston, 1965. Provides a model of the relationship of prayer to the issues in a person's life.

JANE DILLENBERGER, *Style and Content in Christian Art.* Nashville: Abingdon Press, 1965. Through text and picture the author interprets various Christian themes expressed by artists through the centuries.

SHARON N. EMSWILER and THOMAS N. EMSWILER, *Women and Worship: A Guide to Non-Sexist Hymns, Prayers and Liturgies.* New York: Harper & Row, 1974. The book is, as the subtitle promises,

Annotated Bibliography : 195

"a guide to non-sexist hymns, prayers and liturgies." Offers both rationale and examples.

For All God's People: Ecumenical Prayer Cycle. Geneva: World Council of Churches, 1978. Includes meditations related to churches and countries around the world for each day of the year. Useful for private devotions.

PATTY FORBES, *Encountering Prayer and Meditation.* Atlanta: General Assembly Mission Board, Presbyterian Church in the United States, 1979. This is a six-session course for junior high youth offered as part of the Youth Elect Series.

DAG HAMMARSKJÖLD, *Markings.* New York: Alfred A. Knopf, 1964. These are the personal, devotional reflections of the former secretary general of the United Nations.

MARJORIE HOLMES, *Nobody Else Will Listen.* Garden City, N.Y.: Doubleday, 1973. The book is subtitled "A Girl's Conversations with God" and offers insight into the life of a teenage girl.

THOMAS R. KELLY, *A Testament of Devotion.* New York: Harper & Row, 1941. This is a classic map of the territory of the personal devotional life.

The Order for the Celebration of Holy Baptism. Consultation on Church Union. Cincinnati: Forward Movement Publications, 1973. Ten denominations have explored unity together in the consultation, and this book reflects their agreed-upon text for a service of baptism.

WILLIAM R. PARKER and ELAINE ST. JOHNS, *Prayer Can Change Your Life.* New York: Prentice-Hall, 1957. The authors reflect upon personal experience and scientific data to make a case for prayer in one's life.

Prayers We Have in Common: Agreed Liturgical Texts Proposed by the International Consultation on English Texts. Philadelphia: Fortress Press, 1975. This booklet is the product of long-term ecumenical conversation about the appropriate form of the most universal Christian prayers and creeds.

ARLENE SWIDLER, ed., *Sistercelebrations: Nine Worship Experiences.* Philadelphia: Fortress Press, 1974. Offers the text for corporate worship services for a variety of occasions.

CHARLES FRANCIS WHISTON, *Teach Us to Pray.* New York: Pilgrim Press, 1949. Provides a rather full look at the meaning, forms, and types of prayer.

Word, Bread, Cup. Consultation on Church Union. Cincinnati: Forward Movement Publications, 1978. This is a resource for planning and carrying out Holy Communion. It includes background material, orders of worship, and communion texts as agreed upon by members of the consultation.

CHAPTER 4 SYMBOLS AND SEASONS OF
THE CHRISTIAN YEAR

KEITH BOYER and CAROLYN BOYER, *Harvest/Thanksgiving*. New
York: United Church Press, A Living the Word Resource published for Christian Education: Shared Approaches, 1979. Provides
intergenerational resources to learn about and celebrate both
Thanksgiving and the Jewish feast of Booths (Sukkoth).

GEORGE FERGUSON, *Signs and Symbols in Christian Art*. New York:
Oxford University Press, A Galaxy Book, 1979. This is a superb
book that provides background on a variety of symbols. It is
illustrated with symbols and black and white reproductions of a
number of Renaissance paintings.

PATRICIA ROBBENNOLT and ROGER ROBBENNOLT, *Pentecost Planning
Guide*. New York: United Church Press, A Living the Word Resource published for Christian Education: Shared Approaches,
1978. This is a how-to resource to help a congregation to plan
intergenerationally to celebrate Pentecost.

TRUDY VANDER HAAR, *Advent*. New York: United Church Press,
A Living the Word Resource published for Christian Education:
Shared Approaches, 1977. This is a manual to help a congregation
plan intergenerationally for the celebration of Advent.

CHAPTER 5 ENVIRONMENT FOR WORSHIP

Journal of Current Social Issues, Fall 1978. United Church Board
for Homeland Ministries, 132 West 31st Street, New York, New
York 10001. This issue of the *Journal* reports on the May 1978
International Convocation on the Arts, Religion, Architecture,
and the Environment, in San Antonio. The issue is full of insights into the interplay of art and religion.

EDWARD A. SOVIK, *Architecture for Worship*. Minneapolis: Augsburg
Publishing House, 1973. An imaginative architect describes his
craft, dealing with both theoretical and practical elements.

MILDRED C. WIDBER and S. TURNER RITENOUR, *Focus: Building for
Christian Education*. New York: Pilgrim Press, 1969. This is a
comprehensive discussion of the elements in planning for and
developing educational space. The book is nicely illustrated.

CHAPTER 6 THE BIBLE IN WORSHIP

WALTER BRUEGGEMANN, *The Bible Makes Sense*. Atlanta: John Knox
Press, 1977. A sound biblical scholar and excellent teacher takes
the reader on a journey into the Bible's words, symbols, and world.

JOAN HAUGERUD, *The Word for Us: The Gospels of John and Mark, Epistles to the Romans and the Galatians.* Seattle: Coalition on Women and Religion, 1977. This is a restatement, in inclusive language, of the text for these four New Testament books. Illustrates well the problems and possibilities.

Human Sexuality: A Preliminary Study/The United Church of Christ. New York: United Church Press, 1977. The second chapter provides solid background in biblical interpretation and insights into an androgynous understanding.

The Interpreter's Bible. Nashville: Abingdon Press, 1951f. This twelve-volume work lists both the King James and the Revised Standard version texts for each verse in the Bible. It provides background on textual origins and meanings as well as commentary about contemporary meaning.

The Interpreter's Dictionary of the Bible. Nashville: Abingdon Press, 1962. This four-volume work provides in-depth insights into particular biblical words, events, concepts, and practices.

Language About God in Liturgy and Scripture, A Study Guide. Philadelphia: The Geneva Press, 1980. Provides a six-session guide to help adults or youth deal with God language. Includes two interesting background articles.

The Lectionary. Princeton, N.J.: Consultation on Church Union, 1974. This is a listing of biblical passages for each Sunday in the year that have been agreed upon by the members of the consultation representing ten denominations.

CLINTON MORRISON, *An Analytic Concordance to the Revised Standard Version of the New Testament.* Philadelphia: Westminster Press, 1979. Provides a listing of key New Testament words and phrases. It is almost an index of the testament. A feature of the book is its listing of Greek word equivalents.

Nelson's Complete Concordance to the Revised Standard Version Bible. New York: Thomas Nelson, Inc., 1978. This extensive volume includes almost every word that appears in the RSV Bible and gives a listing of where to find it.

LETTY M. RUSSELL, ed., *The Liberating Word: A Guide to Non-Sexist Interpretation of the Bible.* Philadelphia: Westminster Press, 1976. The book gives background on sexism in biblical translation and offers guidelines on how to use the Bible to overcome cultural bias.

PHYLLIS TRIBLE, *God and the Rhetoric of Sexuality.* Philadelphia: Fortress Press, 1978. The author is an Old Testament scholar who interprets the feminist, androgynous stream in the Bible and relates it to issues of sexuality.

CHAPTER 7 MUSIC IN WORSHIP

RICHARD K. AVERY and DONALD S. MARSH, *The Avery and Marsh Songbook.* Port Jervis, N.Y.: Proclamation Publications, 1977. This is a collection of sixty-one songs and hymns made popular by this liturgical/music team.

GROSVENOR COOPER, *Learning to Listen: A Handbook for Music.* Chicago: University of Chicago Press, Phoenix Books, 1962. A short, basic review of the terms and structure of music.

A Guide to Music for the Church Year. Minneapolis: Augsburg Publishing House, fourth edition, 1974. Helps the worship planner choose appropriate music for each season of the Christian year.

MADELINE D. INGRAM, *Organizing and Directing Children's Choirs.* Nashville: Abingdon Press, 1959. A standard review of how to develop and maintain children's choirs in the church.

HUGH M. MILLER, *Introduction to Music.* New York: Barnes & Noble, College Outline Series, 1958. A standard college outline text. The work provides a quick overview of the structure and elements of musical form.

ALBERT C. RONANDER and ETHEL PORTER, *A Guide to the Pilgrim Hymnal.* New York: Pilgrim Press, 1966. This book is correlated with the *Pilgrim Hymnal,* first published by Pilgrim Press in 1958. It offers background information on each hymn in the hymnal.

ERIK ROUTLEY, *Music in the Church.* Boston: Crescendo Publishing Co., second revised edition, 1970. Routley is a veteran church musician who writes of his craft.

H. AUGUSTINE SMITH, *Lyric Religion: The Romance of Immortal Hymns.* Old Tappan, N.J.: Fleming H. Revell, 1931. Provides historical and interpretive material on a number of well-known hymns.

CHAPTER 8 MOVEMENT IN WORSHIP

DOUG ADAMS, *Congregational Dancing in Christian Worship.* Austin, Tex.: Sharing Co., revised edition, 1977. Provides historical and theoretical interpretation of dance as part of the congregation's liturgy.

DOUG ADAMS and JUDITH ROCK, *Biblical Criteria in Modern Dance: Modern Dance as a Prophetic Form.* Austin, Tex.: Sharing Co., 1979. Contends that there is both biblical style and biblical form, and illustrates the ways in which dance interprets the Bible.

CARLA DE SOLA, *Learning Through Dance.* New York: Paulist Press, 1974. Combines solid interpretation of dance movements and elements with religious ideas. This is an extremely practical book.

———, *The Spirit Moves: A Handbook of Dance and Prayer.* Washington, D.C.: Liturgical Conference, 1977. A beautiful book that explores a combination of practical approaches to doing dance and vital aesthetic theory. Relates dance to the eucharist, Christian seasons, special occasions, and scripture.

JUDITH ROCK, *Theology in the Shape of Dance: Using Dance in Worship and in Theological Process.* Austin, Tex.: Sharing Co., 1978. This pamphlet reviews basic theological and practical issues in using dance in worship.

MARGARET FISK TAYLOR, *A Time to Dance: Symbolic Movement in Worship.* Austin, Tex.: Sharing Co., revised edition, 1976. Provides interpretation of the why and how of dance in worship. Includes solid historical background. Offers illustrations of passages or works to use in symbolic movement.

Worship and the Arts, Liturgical Dance. Joint Office of Worship, 1044 Alta Vista Road, Louisville, Kentucky 40205. One of three kits prepared by the United Presbyterian and the Southern Presbyterian joint worship office. Marge Champion was a key resource in developing this kit, which includes an 11-minute 16 mm film.

CHAPTER 9 EDUCATIONAL DEVELOPMENT AND WORSHIP

BRUNO BETTELHEIM, *The Uses of Enchantment: The Meaning and Importance of Fairy Tales.* New York: Random House, 1977. The author, a distinguished child development researcher, interprets the meaning of fairy tales in relation to children's experience. The interpretation is heavily Freudian.

ERIK H. ERIKSON, *Childhood and Society.* New York: W.W. Norton, 1964. This is Erikson's classic work in which he develops his theory of psychosocial tasks for each age. Insightful book that is engaging to read.

———, *Toys and Reasons: Stages in the Ritualization of Experience.* New York: W.W. Norton, 1977. The human development researcher who coined the phrase "identity crisis" relates stages to rites of passage and celebration.

JAMES FOWLER and SAM KEEN, *Life-Maps: Conversations on the Journey of Faith.* Waco, Tex.: Word Books, 1978. A good overview of Fowler's insights into faith development.

PAULO FREIRE, *Pedagogy of the Oppressed.* New York: Seabury Press, 1970. This is Freire's seminal work as he relates education to the processes of human liberation and community-building. Symbolic language is very important for him.

LAWRENCE KOHLBERG, "Stage and Sequence: The Cognitive-Developmental Approach to Socialization," *Handbook of Socialization Theory and Research,* ed. by David A. Goslin. Chicago: Rand McNally, 1969. The author's theory and research on how moral development happens are summarized here.

DANIEL J. LEVINSON et al., *The Seasons of a Man's Life*. New York: Alfred A. Knopf, 1978. Levinson studied forty men over a long period of time and developed a theory of stages and seasons based upon what they told him.

C. ELLIS NELSON, *Where Faith Begins*. Atlanta: John Knox Press, 1967. A religious educator who has studied human development extensively describes the processes within the life of a congregation.

GWEN KENNEDY NEVILLE and JOHN H. WESTERHOF, III, *Learning Through Liturgy*. New York: Seabury Press, 1978. Westerhoff, from the perspective of an educator, and Neville, from an anthropology perspective, look at rites, community, and human development.

PENELOPE WASHBOURN, *Becoming Woman: The Quest for Spiritual Wholeness in Female Experience*. New York: Harper & Row, 1977. Provides insight into the key transitional periods in women's lives and identifies related religious meanings.